CONSUMED

THE NEED FOR COLLECTIVE CHANGE: COLONIALISM, CLIMATE CHANGE, AND CONSUMERISM

AJA BARBER

balance

NEW YORK   BOSTON

Balance
Hachette Book Group
1290 Avenue of the Americas, New York, NY 10104
grandcentralpublishing.com
twitter.com/grandcentralpub

Originally published in Great Britain in September 2021 by Brazen, an imprint of Octopus Publishing Group Ltd, a Hachette UK Company
First North American edition: October 2021

Balance is an imprint of Grand Central Publishing. The Balance name and logo are trademarks of Hachette Book Group, Inc.

The publisher is not responsible for websites (or their content) that are not owned by the publisher.

The Hachette Speakers Bureau provides a wide range of authors for speaking events. To find out more, go to www.hachettespeakersbureau.com or call (866) 376-6591.

Library of Congress Control Number: 2021940567

ISBNs: 978-1-5387-0984-9 (trade paperback), 978-1-5387-0985-6 (ebook)

Printed in the United States of America

LSC-C

Printing 1, 2021

To the grandmothers I've known in this lifetime who have taught me so much and lived more sustainably than anyone I know— Emma, Catherine, and Ann.

(Grammy, you would be so proud, my goodness, you'd tell everyone.)

CONTENTS

CONTENTS

NOTE ON THE US EDITION

Hello there, Reader,

I'm an American but I'm based in London. What that means is some of the language and rhetoric you'll see here might pertain to the UK and some might pertain to the US. You get both—lucky you! Sometimes I code switch; sometimes I use facts and figures from both places in the same section, sometimes I talk about one or the other. Language is flexible, and all the stats here are verifiable. Roll with me!

MY LETTER TO THE FAST FASHION CEOS

Hello there, my dudes,*

Aja Barber here.

I'm one of many of us with platforms, telling my following and anyone who will listen to *not* support your brands and your businesses anymore and to seek alternative options (if they can). I hope you read this book, and I hope you know that I have no plans of stopping until something changes. Or I die. But the women in my family tend to live long, healthy lives, so I might just be here for a while. That is, unless the climate emergency kills us all (enjoy your underground bunkers, dudes).

I wanted to let you know that, upon publication of this book, I will have donated $10,000 of my own hard-earned money to

---

*It's safe to address you as "dudes" because 95 percent of you are men (according to "The Route to the Top 2018" report by Heidrick and Struggles), which is frankly a problem, but that's for another book.

both garment worker unions and organizations at the end of *your* supply chain. I am not a billionaire (but most of you are). I am not even a millionaire (but most of you are). I'm an individual who put way too much of my money into your pockets for far too long, when it should have been in the garment worker's pocket *all along*.

But back to you.

Every single day, you have plenty of opportunities to do the right thing. And the power with which to do it. And you choose not to.

You could pay more money for your clothing at the factory, agreeing on an absolute minimum for certain items at cost, which would eliminate the race to the bottom globally.

You could give your money directly to garment worker unions and stop union busting.

You could clean up the waterways that your clothing factories are spewing waste into at an accelerating rate.

You could simply choose to make less stuff and stop pushing consumers to buy more of it through manipulative and expensive marketing (and perhaps consider, if you didn't spend those seven- or eight-figure sums on pushing products, where that money could go—yes, you guessed it, to the people who created your products in the first place).

Of course, all of this looks like smaller profit margins for you, but let me tell you, it looks like a better and more sustainable world for everyone else.

We all know this planet has far too much stuff, and that's a problem you've created—one that is harming the people, the climate, and the planet.

Every year, month, day, and even hour that you choose not

to do these things, you are *willingly* turning away from the problem you have created and profited almightily from. Some of you have so much money that you could give away 90 percent of it and never run out of money in your lifetime.

So that's what I challenge you to do.

Use *your* money to clean up *your* mess. Use your enormous fortunes to make this system better for everyone. Step away from this slash-and-burn cycle. Stop with the "cute" recycling bins in stores, which your market research has taught you only incentivize consumers to buy more. Cut it out with the sustainable lines that account for less than 1 percent of your business. Reform your *entire* business from top to bottom—from how you treat people at the bottom right through to the growth targets you set yourself. Think about other growth targets, like 0 percent carbon emissions. First person to use their own money to do this wins, and I'll stay off your back (until you do something else crappy). The days of hand-over-fist profit over humanity are over. It's kind of a bad look.

I still believe you might have a smidgen of humanity left in you, behind those piles of money you are so keen to grow, with no real purpose other than capitalist ambition. So, prove it. Because here's the thing: you can't buy integrity.

Now read on.

INTRODUCTION

"Every consumer has the right to know who produces their clothing and under what conditions, whether it be labor conditions or environmental, just like the ingredients written on the food packaging that you buy."
—*Anannya Bhattacharjee, Asia Floor Wage Alliance,*
and Garment and Allied Workers Union

Welcome to *Consumed*. This is a book about stuff (particularly apparel) and why we need less of it, and what information you need in order to climb out of this mess.

The book is divided into two sections: part 1 is everything you need to know, but maybe didn't (I mean, I didn't know either until a short while ago) about how we got here, and why this problem is historical and endemic and tied down to oppression along the way. It will get heavy, but we will hear from the people who need to be heard.

In part 2 I address you. Hi, consumer of stuff! It isn't your fault that overconsumption has become a part of our culture. The likelihood is that you do it, just like I did, because you've been taught to. Who else is going to change this system other than you and me?

CONSUMED

PART ONE

1

SUSTAINABILITY AND ME

How did I get into this conversation in the first place?

From a very young age, I understood the power of sartorial choice. When I got to high school, my passion had turned from an interest in fitting in through material items and consumption into a genuine love of fashion, but I was also very aware of my placement in life. I knew there was very little room for Black girls in the fashion industry, but my progressive (though not *that* progressive) parents had taken the approach to education that many an ethnic parent has taken. I knew that in our society you need a degree to do anything so, gosh darn it, I did my time. And even though it was abundantly clear to me that working in fashion was so out of my reach (I mean, at the time, the Parsons School of Design in New York was three times the cost of my yearly university tuition; it seemed like a no-win game), that didn't stop me from trying. I always kept my eye out, read everything I could, and kept an ear to the ground. I began to find my people through various fashion boards, where commenters from all over the world would weigh in on various subjects and give insight into fashion trends I had very little access to in northern Virginia.

During my sophomore year of university, my older sister (similar to many other twenty-somethings) decided to make a move to New York City, and I helped her, driving up with her and another friend. Once we had settled her into her dingy and overpriced new living space in Queens, we set out into Greenwich Village for food, drinks, and debauchery. That night, we ended up in a bar on the Lower East Side, catching up with a friend of a friend whom we happened to bump into on the street. At the next table over, there was a birthday party going on, and I quickly spotted an editor of a magazine I used to read, *Lucky*. Never one to miss a moment, I slid up to her and said, "I think I know you from a magazine. You work for *Lucky*, right?" It was Andrea Linett, the founding creative director of *Lucky*, and she was kind and gracious, and she told me to get in touch if I was interested in interning. I didn't even realize how generous she was being at the time, but I did think to myself: *Fuck an internship, I need a job. How does anyone work for free, no matter how fun it may be?* I'm just acknowledging this now, but that was the beginning of me questioning the mere idea of internships (despite the fact that I would, in fact, intern in the future; see p. 15).

While the concept of interning seemed to me to make it impossible, I still regret not emailing to stay in touch. I also still remember that emotion of being starstruck and feeling as though anything can happen in cities. You can meet a fashion editor you really admire on a random night out on the Lower East Side. But that's totally why people who live in certain metropolitan areas, and have a certain socioeconomic status, always have an advantage over those that don't when it comes to certain industries. Because you have to be in the right place for things to line up, even if by happenstance.

One thing my parents agreed that I would be allowed to do was study abroad and, lucky for me, my school had an abundance of programs to pick from. I made a list of my top cities (Paris, Rome, Tokyo, London), listing the pros and the cons of the programs, but eventually settled on London, because I already had friends in the city (from traveling) and already spoke the language. (This is honestly one of the most sloth-like, most American things I've ever typed about myself...but no one can drag you for it if you drag yourself—just kidding, drag away.) As someone who's always been aware of social settings, I was quick to realize that going to study in a foreign city where I already had a handful of friends would only help me to get the most out of the experience.

THE RUDE YEARS

I visited London in February of 2000, and it looked like a very optimistic, bright place. Electronic music was king, and London was the place to be. I remember the excitement of riding the Tube. I remember how everyone in London looked far cooler than my peers in the US, and I remember the casual attitude toward sex, drugs, and alcohol among my peers, which seemed alluring. I was home. I had to get back here as soon as possible, even if I couldn't attend school here full-time.

London was happening.

Despite being a pretty hard worker, I was never a scholarly

type, and the only way I got through university was thinking about all the things I would do once I was able to leave. I frankly couldn't wait for my life to begin, and a semester abroad in London was exactly the way forward.

My school offered a "Work Abroad" program, and that sounded right up my alley. You mean they were going to give me credit to lay the groundwork for a career in another country? *I'll take that, thank you.* But trying to work out where I could *work* and make it *work* was a whole different issue...

A few summers earlier, passing through London Heathrow with my dad and my sisters, I had dipped into a WH Smith in the airport terminal to pick up an armload full of British fashion magazines. They introduced me to brands I hadn't heard of, but the real kicker was that UK fashion magazines always came with little extras. That summer, a magazine that is no longer in circulation and had been reissued from the sixties, *Nova*, caught my eye. They were offering a weird little tank top. Yup. That's how abundant clothing is and was.

Once aboard our flight from London to Barcelona, I tore into my stash and began to flip through *Nova*. It had good fashion layouts and articles from notable people in London, and on one page there was an advertisement full of fun young people wearing bright clothing adorned with beautiful minimal line drawings. It was a barbecue scene on a rooftop. *Why are Londoners just so fun?* I thought to myself. The advertisement was for a little streetwear brand called Rude, and I was immediately obsessed. What I didn't know at the time was that the people in that advertisement weren't just models, they were two people who would become two of my very best friends, Rupert and Abi.

While I sat on that flight, scheming about how I could jump into this ad and join the party, I was cementing a crucial bit of my future that would bring me to this moment where I am today, sitting on my couch in South London, typing to you. Because some things are just meant to be.

From my history of letter writing to CEOs and companies (when I was a child, I was the go-to letter writer for my family whenever we had something we needed to say to a corporation; this also made me realize how much money these corporations had to give away), I knew how to craft a good letter. I had searched the Rude website and found a contact email for a person named Abi. I imagine it looked something like this:

Hello! My name is Aja Barber. I'm a student in the US who has the fantastic opportunity to do an internship in the UK for a semester. I'm a big fan of your brand. Currently I am in school, but I also do promotions for a record label. [I did...I was the DC street-team rep for Astralwerks, and it was great, all the free gigs and free CDs you could want.] In exchange for all the free clothing of my choosing, I would love to come and work for your brand as your in-house PR. Please find my attached résumé. Look forward to hearing from you.

And Abi wrote back something like:

Great! When can you start?

I couldn't believe it! This cool brand that I was really into was going to let me come and work in their head office? Well, it's all about moxie, kids. (And a lot of things lining up for me in the right way...some of which came from moxie, some of which came from a boatload of privilege.) Moxie is a funny thing: not too much of it, because that turns people off, but using just enough in the right moment can be one of the better decisions of your life. Seventeen years later, Rupert told me that when Abi announced that she had agreed to take on some random student from the United States off of one email, he asked her, "Okay, but are you mad? Some weird American writes you an email and you're like 'sure'?"

I knew several families who lived in London, but I knew of one family in Hackney whom I always had a lot of fun with, and I decided I would ask them if I could rent a spare room for the semester. I didn't know much about Hackney, besides the fact that people said it was "a bit rough," which sounded perfect. I wanted the real experience. If I was going to go to a place, I really wanted to live it and immerse myself. And moving to Navarino Road would provide just that experience (today, Navarino Road is actually a pretty upmarket location, but at the time people still called it "rough"). Upon hearing back that, yes, they did have a room, and I was free to take it for a small fee, I clasped my hands happily. It was all coming together.

Roughly two months later I sat aboard *the most turbulent* flight to this day I've ever flown on. The jumbo jet bounced up and down like a tennis ball against the night sky's racket. I was pretty sure I was going to die, and I thought to myself, *God, if I survive this, I know London will be worth my while.* By the time the turbulence decided to stop making me pray for my life, I peered out of the plane window and was totally in love. I've never felt more like "I'm home" to a place I had never spent extended time in. Sometimes you just know.

The weekend before I started at Rude, I went to scope where exactly the studio was based so I wouldn't be late on my first day (gotta make a good impression). In those days, Spitalfields Market existed pre-development and gentrification. The neighborhood—Shoreditch—was, frankly, rough. Half the buildings were abandoned, and one could describe Shoreditch circa 2003 as a post-industrial wasteland. But it was also a total playground for creative people, and man, did they flock there. My partner once described Shoreditch then versus now; he said: "When you were hanging out in Shoreditch, it was kind of wanky but full of beautiful people, and some of them might be wearing lampshades on their heads as part of an artsy music video. Today it's still wanky but full of beautiful people, and so many of them are posing for Instagram shots with iced coffee because no artist can afford it anymore."

Shoreditch has always been a bit of a joke for the hipsters, and I was happily one of them. When I arrived at the Rude building the following Monday morning on a damp January day, I rang the buzzer and was let in. This studio was like no place I had ever seen before in my life. I could tell immediately it was a place of creativity and joy. I couldn't believe I got to work there.

WORK PLACEMENTS

The sum of what I know about clothing production was learned at Rude. The advantage of doing a work placement with a small company is that you get to have a hand in everything. You get to be present at meetings and learn about the ins and outs in a way that bigger companies rarely provide. Rupert and Abi were generous when it came to including me in interesting discussions, and they were good at giving power to those within the company and delegating responsibility and credit. One graphic designer had a lot of work on her plate and showed me how to cut out images on Illustrator to help her with the catalogue for spring/summer 2004. I had never even opened Illustrator before, and there I was using it and getting a quick crash course. I was invited to my first ever trade show in Battersea Park, so I could understand the full process of how a small streetwear brand meets buyers and sells to different vendors.

When Rude opened a store on nearby Hanbury Street, I learned how to stain floors (sometimes I still wander into that shop today, look down at the well-worn floors, and smile to myself, remembering that I did that eighteen years ago). In the store you could get any of their designs printed onto a t-shirt, or use a design of your own, and they also sold a main line of clothes. One of my favorite details of all the Rude collections was that all the clothing from a single season matched with the other pieces. You could pair literally every item together and make a bunch of different outfits. I call it "getting dressed quickly and effectively."

Getting the store ready was a feat. I talked on the phone with countless PRs ahead of our launch and became known as "that chatty American girl." Rude had a ton of ready-made designs with simple line drawings, which was our signature. But our idea of printing made-to-order t-shirts was actually pretty out-of-the-box, and few people were doing it at the time. (Today, almost twenty years later, a famous chain has a similar operation at their Oxford Street shop, but their price point is far cheaper than Rude's because of exploitation within their supply chain.) When your Rude t-shirt was ready to go, we placed it in our signature pizza box.

All of Rude's clothing was made in Portugal, ethically, and the quality was impeccable. Most of my favorite pieces were made from cotton or linen, and the garments I acquired during my time at Rude I would go on to wear for the rest of my twenties until I could no longer fit a size UK14/US10. There were some mistakes, though, because when the factory messed up orders, they really messed up. One season they used cheap zippers in the dresses and skirts instead of the requested YKK zippers. YKK (which stands for Yoshida Kogyo Kabushikikaisha) is a Japanese company and the largest zipper manufacturer in the world. While monopolies aren't always the best thing for a healthy economy, you'd be hard pressed to find anyone who wouldn't say YKK's zippers are sturdy and reliable. That entire season we got tons of skirts returned with broken zippers. But the absolute worst was when some poor woman got stuck in one of our dresses in the fitting room. Abi and I ended up having to cut her out of the dress, which couldn't have been a fun experience for her.

The moral of the story: don't cut corners. (This was something the factory decided to do.) But it's little things that you think don't matter that absolutely do and can ruin your selling season for a portion of your inventory. Even if you get your money back from the factory, that's still money lost for an entire season, which you can't pay your staff or yourselves out of. This was a lesson in quality which always stuck with me.

But there were also lessons in sustainability that I learned. The thing is, the legendary waste that we hear about within the fashion industry is completely counterproductive, and the industry learns nothing from the ways in which ethical brands have always operated. It's not cool or practical to waste tons of fabric and, if your budget is limited, you can't *afford* to waste it. Rude was a waste not, want not operation. When there was a leftover bolt of brown cotton denim-like fabric delivered to the office, from a sample that was never put into production, that bolt of fabric hung out in the studio until Abi decided what we were going to do with it. Throwing it away was never on the table. Eventually we put the bolt to use.

One day Abi decided we should make some bags to give away with purchases in our shop. At the time no one was giving away free tote bags because much of the world was still championing plastic. Of course, we have a free tote problem now, but...if it's made of the leftover end of a fabric roll (deadstock), I still see no problem with it.

Another trainee and I were put to work making the bags. We came up with a very quick design that took five minutes to zip through on a sewing machine. They were tacky looking but charming, with fabric fringe hanging off the sides. Then we had an idea. We had learned that when you screen-print, there's often a lot of ink left over on your screen. If you're just washing the screen immediately in between colors and prints, you're actually washing a lot of that extra ink straight down the drain. We would take those bits of fabric that would be turned into tote bags and allow the screen-printer to print on them using leftover ink on the screen. You'd end up with one of our signature prints on your free shabby tote bag. No one was really doing this sort of thing at the time, and it was a bit of an extra treat, which would always delight customers.

Mostly, I learned how small brands often operate on razor-thin margins with their cash flow, and how hard it is sometimes to just make it work. Doing wholesale with big-name department stores is beyond challenging for small brands. You've got a pretty tiny window to deliver your inventory to the vendor, and if you miss that window, all your merchandise gets returned to you. Sometimes this can occur halfway through the "selling season," which can make it difficult for you to figure out how to sell additional pieces you hadn't planned on having in your possession (this point can also be used in the conversation about moving toward a seasonless fashion calendar—see chapter 4). Oh, and a big department store can reject your goods for any reason at any time.

Rude was the first job I had ever had that I actually missed once my time was up. As cheesy as it sounds, my friends at Rude had become my London family. Big corporations love to refer to their workforce and employees as "family" because it makes it easier to get away with workplace abuse and to place guilt on employees to work harder in a job that often offers little to no upward movement whatsoever. Whenever a bigger company refers to their employees as "family," I always shudder. If it's so much of a family, why not make wages more evenly distributed throughout the entire business, instead of having a bunch of millionaires and billionaires in upper management and minimum-wage workers (and less if we're counting garment workers) at the bottom?

But the thing that touched me most, which I only discovered recently, was that Abi had spoken to the company lawyer to look into how challenging it would be to sponsor me, so I could return and work for the company full-time after I graduated from school the following year. Unfortunately, sponsoring folks to come join your company from outside of the UK (and the US, too, for that matter) is notoriously difficult if you don't have piles of money and aren't a big company. This is another time when I question what makes a "skilled" worker. I think personally the UK could do with a few less finance people working in Canary Wharf, but this issue never seems to be a problem for the banks. Which forces the question, what sort of labor do we value in our society? Especially with regard to who gets to immigrate for work opportunities and who doesn't.

Anyway, after a thoroughly fruitful and frankly life-changing time spent in the UK, making friends and having super-memorable experiences, it was time for me to pack my bags (full of clothes from my new identity as an East London wanker) and be dragged onto a plane home to the US, where I had a full year of university waiting before graduating.

When I returned home, I found I had never been so miserable before in my life. I had found my people for the first time ever. I cried for days. I missed my friends, I missed my life, I missed the constant buzz of creativity, and nothing else would suffice. But it didn't seem like a very viable future for a Black girl from Virginia...and there was no fashion industry in Washington, DC, where I felt that I fit in. My dreams had fully reached harder than my bandwidth.

I had, however, discovered another world happening online, which connected those who loved fashion with other fashion lovers all over the world. It was called "fashion blogging." There was a handful of blogs that I read every day, and it was exciting to watch people go from "fashion blogger" to "sitting front row at the shows." Many people I respect in the industry today got their start blogging. And reading those blogs kept me going while I gathered myself and realized I had to give fashion a crack again. But I had no idea how. I began to realize it was time to move away from home again. I had licked my wounds enough, and I was ready to get back in the world, taking uncalculated risks. Fashion magazines were starting to go digital, and everyone was shifting toward online content. Many magazines were producing their own online video shorts to put on their websites. Since I already had experience in television, I knew that I could easily be of use in many of these operations. I narrowed it down to my favorite magazines and started the process of randomly emailing again. How hard could it be? Turns out very hard to get paid, but not too hard to get an internship. I soon found a nice unpaid position for myself at a magazine I had read for years. It was time for a new adventure, in a new city...New York City.

THE NEW YORK YEARS

No one can ever prepare you for the New York City roommate hunt. Finding a place to live is exhausting, tiresome, and burdensome, no matter where you are; I feel for anyone who has to move at any time for any reason. But finding a place in New York City is the Thunderdome of roommating. It is an often fruitless search of trying to suss out who's an absolute weirdo, while simultaneously trying to give off vibes that *you* are not a weirdo. It is an endless tap dance of trying to seem both laidback and impressive. It felt like all the worst job interviews I had ever experienced, and this was all for the honor of paying too much money to live with someone I didn't particularly want to live with. Sometimes you can tell from the Craigslist ad that you might just wake up handcuffed to your bed in a room of stuffed animals. I must have seen twenty-five different rooms. Some situations were deeply competitive, and you walked away knowing that you just weren't cool enough to be selected. Some were super-weird. I went to see a room in an abandoned squat that looked downright squalid...and that shit was not cheap. They wanted $850 a month to wear shoes indoors because of the rats. One girl who was moving out actually offered me the room but then called me later and begged me not to move in, because the roommates were actually awful and she thought I seemed like a nice person. I'm still grateful for that call.

But when the stars align and you find just the right place...I found a beautiful, airy loft on a second floor with white wooden floors, which was both clean and tastefully decorated, and "affordable." To this day, it's my favorite place I have ever lived in. It was $950 a month, but I had saved $15,000 from living with my parents and working at a design firm. I also planned on still working in television in New York City to supplement my non-paying magazine internship and pay for things like lunch in SoHo. That year I ate so much two-dollar falafel that I couldn't eat falafel for years.

UNPAID INTERNSHIPS

So, if everyone has to work unpaid internships in the magazine world in the hope of getting a paying job eventually...how does anyone who can't afford to work for free manage to get any-where in the magazine world? **The answer is: they don't.** The fashion and magazine world perpetuates and supports a certain class of society getting into the room and excludes everyone else. If we do not discontinue the practice of unpaid internship, we will continue to have industries where only upper- and middle-class people can hold jobs and have opportunities. While there

> "Humans are not consumables. Pay your workers."

has been some movement in government legislation to stamp out this practice, it still persists. It sucks, and I hate it. Humans are not consumables. Pay your workers.

Additionally, I recognize that not everyone can just move back in with their parents and then work really, really hard so they can have the chance to pack their bags and move to a bigger city in order to work really hard for free. It's all so incredibly unfair, and I hate it. I hated that I didn't refuse to participate in all this sooner. But if I didn't, I probably wouldn't be sitting here writing this book. Every shit experience helps me to see all the problems I talk about in my spaces today. I'm not grateful for them, but they have played their part in making me the person I am today. I'm just sorry I wasn't in a place to call bullshit sooner, because this system of unpaid internships is utter bullshit and *everybody* knows it.

The biggest dealbreaker of all is healthcare, in my humble opinion. The National Health Service in the UK allows you to chase your dreams in a way that many aren't afforded in the US, ever. I know countless folks who hold on to whatever miserable job they can have, just because being uninsured and ill is a nightmare of epic proportions. Not insured in America? Imagine your appendix decides to rupture. You're looking at $15,000 for the hospital bill. (I know because it happened to someone I knew, who was lucky enough to have parents who could help.) There were brief moments in my adult life when I was uninsured, and I was very fortunate to have nothing happen to me during those times. But had I had an accident, I could have been in debt for the rest of my life. The Affordable Care Act really changed my life, and I'll always be grateful for that. Not worrying about how I'm going to be insured and cared for in the UK is a privilege.

Back in New York, on the first day of my internship at what I'll call the Unnamed Magazine Like All the Others, I took the train to SoHo and found I quickly got tired of the constantly packed streets. When I arrived at Greene Street, I spoke to the receptionist and took the elevator to the fifth floor. The office I found myself in was frankly cramped and underwhelming. It was one of those open-plan type offices that was buzzing with energy... bad, negative energy. What had I signed myself up for?

I assisted in the TV department. I didn't realize that the "department" consisted of one computer with Final Cut Pro (still the bane of my existence) and one camera (later we would acquire a second camera).

I'll never forget my very white superior telling me that a world-famous store was named Trash Vaudeville. It's not. The East Village punk emporium is called Trash and Vaudeville, and the manager, Jimmy Webb, was a legend who remembered my face whenever I went in (he had that way of making people feel special). Imagine how infuriating it is to be corrected about an establishment you're very familiar with. When she finally stood corrected, there wasn't a moment of humility there, or even "Wow, am I obnoxious!" That was what it was like being one of the few Black faces at a very white magazine.

I actually hated it when white people caught on to anything I liked that was considered a "white interest," because they would try to "whitesplain" that very thing to me, even though I had probably been enjoying that thing long before they even knew of said thing's existence. I started to notice that if I expressed an interest that other people didn't prescribe as belonging to the tight little box I was supposed to be put in as a Black teenager in the 1990s, it couldn't possibly be an interest that I could claim as my own. It generally felt like, if I liked a thing—anything—as long as no one else liked it, it was my thing to just enjoy. But, Lord, if white people liked it, get ready to be quizzed on whether or not you truly deserved to like it. White men often do this to white women. But white people also do this to everyone who isn't white. I don't make up the rules, that's just how things are!

My store-name-correcting superior was mostly out of the office, flying around the world, and would come home and deposit handfuls of receipts for me to file and hours of footage for me to watch and log for the first cut of edits. Being that there was only one computer for our department, only one of us could work at a time, which made the entire system utterly dysfunctional. I had hoped that I could pitch more ideas for compelling content, but everyone at the magazine was underpaid, overworked, and constantly stressed. I also began to truly understand the notion of turf guarding. A lot of folks operated under the assumption that if they hadn't come up with the good idea themselves, you had better not mention it.

It was also largely frowned upon to speak to people from other departments about anything, especially if you were a lowly intern. And heaven forbid you speak to the Editor. Though the

Editor wasn't exactly someone I went out of my way to speak to. There was a certain insincerity and emptiness, especially in the Editor's Letters, which soon came to light for me. I remember thinking, *What sort of navel-gazing drivel is this?* when my magazine would fall open to the Editor's Letter.

Magazines and celebrities have a symbiotic, mutually beneficial relationship. Celebrities don't get tons of money for appearing in magazines. Contrary to popular belief, they don't even get to keep the clothes, unless the designer decides to gift them (or the celebrity decides to steal them). The samples they're wearing are often worth thousands of dollars, so stealing the clothes is really bad form, but when you reach a certain level of fame sometimes you can get away with a lot before anyone holds you to account. Either way, there's not much in it for the celebrity except for the press side. The magazine gets cover sales, which keeps the lights on. I personally won't buy a magazine if a celebrity I don't like is on the cover, and I think most people should take that approach. Regardless, the magazine is consuming the celebrity, the celeb is consuming the relevance, and we're all consuming... well, a lot of different things, but we're mostly being sold to at every turn of the page, as many magazines are made up of mostly advertisements. We are being sold to while buying their product. And that's why you'll never get truly honest reporting on the scope of the fashion industry's problems from traditional fashion magazines. They, too, have a symbiotic relationship with some of the biggest polluters in the industry, as bottom line they're dependent on advertisers' dollars. If you piss off your advertisers, it's going to be a struggle for your publication, even when asking those advertisers to lend you clothing for fashion shoots.

When the management isn't nice—especially to its employees—bad attitude permeates all spaces. This place was so notorious for bad behavior that it was no surprise most of the employees weren't invited to the magazine's monthly launch party, which was an alcohol free-for-all. The irony that they could always find money for a party but never find money for interns…I managed to attend two parties (to work on the video team), and I realized that I could never have a good time in such a mean-spirited environment, no matter how drunk I got once the work was done.

A *hard* guideline for you is to leave any internship that doesn't offer you opportunities to learn or grow. If you aren't learning new things or getting connections, then it's simply not worth doing at all. I wish I had left sooner. But I was determined that I would turn it into a job, so I put my nose to the computer screen and proceeded to be the best at any assignment I was given. I had done a little sleuthing around the office and also found that, out of all the staff, only a few had become paid workers from internships. Mostly, the place just abused people's labor any way they could.

A very informative report by the Sustainable Fashion Initiative, of the Myron E. Ullman Jr. School of Design in Cincinnati, about unpaid internships called "The Dream Will Never Pay Off" in 2020 found that "on average a Fashion Design Student at the University of Cincinnati pays $37,607.50 for the expenses related to their internship experiences." That sounds shockingly accurate. The report also notes that 77.8 percent of those interviewed said they received financial help from family in order to make ends meet while interning. I was shocked to find that some students are forced to take out loans and additional debt (besides student loans) for the "honor" of interning. And on top of that, a graph in the report shows that only 23.6 percent of those interviewed were offered full-time employment. Isn't this supposed to be a stepping stone into the working world or something? The report also tells a narrative of racial exclusion throughout the industry. "BIPOC Interns are often 'othered' due to the significant lack of representation within the industry. More so, Fashion outright excludes BIPOC students, especially those coming from economically marginalized backgrounds, by requiring interns to commit to such high financial costs in order to further their education and career."

The only other Black person I worked with at the magazine was a nice woman in promotions, whose face I met immediately while scanning the sea of white faces upon my first day of stepping into the office (for the record, less than half of New York City's population was white at the time). Once we realized we were on the same page of thinking, *Gee, this place is problematic,* we would shoot each other horrified looks when we witnessed outright racism and general nonsense. I began to always shoot extra images of content that she could use specifically in her department. Anytime she had an errand or needed a hand, I was happy to pitch in. I distinctly remember riding the subway with a massive life-size copy of the magazine on my lap, which had gotten left behind at a party venue. I rode the subway because those cheap fucks would not have expensed a cab for me at any point for any reason. I would find out later that she had broached the topic with upper management of bringing me on and paying me (a zero-hour contract, of course) because I filled many holes...

It doesn't surprise me that the Black person whom I wasn't an intern for was the only person who would vouch for my skill set. She deserved better, and so did I.

Another thing...the magazine expected all the interns take out the trash. Imagine that. However, the interns who considered themselves too good to actually do any work never took out the trash and just looked at the rest of us with utter disdain, so I soon decided that I wasn't going to do it either. Nuh-uh. Hire a janitor, assholes (no shade to janitors, that is good and important work. However, there is such a thing as exploitation).

As I got to know my fellow interns, I also began to realize that I was quite possibly the only one who wasn't being supported by my parents. Many admitted that they had done countless internships in the city, over the course of several years, with no real money or paycheck involved. I finally asked in my naïveté, "But how do you all afford to do this?" And a kindly intern told me: "Most of our parents pay our rent."

I had stumbled into a special sort of hell, and none of it was worth it. I worked nonstop, and I was always tired and *always* hungry. There were days when I would have eaten free food off the street to save a few extra dollars. It was the first time in my life that I had felt actual jealousy over people in relationships, mostly because they had someone to split rent and a bedroom with, and some days, after NYC really beats you up, what you need most is a hug. It was the first time in my life I began to think about the privileges that people in partnerships are granted. During that period of my life there was no time for socializing, or even making friends, and there were few treats... besides iced coffee, because I'm not sure how I would have run

> "It was the first time in my life that I had felt actual jealousy over people in relationships, mostly because they had someone to split rent and a bedroom with, and some days, after NYC really beats you up, what you need most is a hug."

at that pace without caffeine. I had always heard all these things about the magazine industry, but I guess it had to be proved to me that there is basically no real way to get ahead in that space unless you have good connections and privilege, and then you probably didn't even need the job to eat.

When my months of servitude had come to an end, and all I had gotten was a few hard-fought paid days—which took six months to process, even though, according to the law, it should have taken at most ninety days (which meant that if I was dependent on that money to buy my groceries I would surely have been out of luck)—I took my lack of contract employment as a personal failure. Someone else who was better connected than me was hired in my department. I felt beat up and a little lost in a city that didn't seem to like me that much. I really couldn't decide whether to stay in New York City and continue down the path of unpaid employment and working nights and weekends to live or admit defeat and go home.

In the end, I moved yet again into my parents' basement, where I licked my wounds and moped (and worked, because non-rich parents are like, "I'm sorry you're sad, now get a job"). I had heard that leaving New York City does that to a person. But I could finally buy groceries again without worrying about how I would pay for public transportation. (I could even buy a pair of new shoes. New York is very, very hard on your shoes. As is

London.) I began to throw myself into my fashion blog online, as the genre was only continuing to grow and there was something exciting about it, just connecting with other people who loved fashion as much as I did.

I began to question whether perhaps it wasn't entirely failure I felt but relief dressed in a different outfit.

THE BASEMENT YEARS

Blogging came first.

And Instagram came second.

I've made many attempts to participate in the fashion industry; sometimes, not being picked for the first round (or the second round, or even the third round) of something means that later down the line you come back stronger. It's this that has allowed me to feel able to talk about the real issues in the industry today.

Back in the day it was just me, my mom, and my trusty point-and-shoot. If anything came out of my time as a blogger, it was that my mother got *really* good at taking an outfit photo. Or, rather, she stopped cutting off my head, which was progress for her from my childhood in the eighties.

Blogging was a great place to just put that outfit on when you wanted the world to see it and you wanted to be noticed. But as I dove deeper into the world of fashion blogging, I began to feel like I was always struggling to keep up or participate, and it stopped being fun. I was beginning to realize it was just a new way to consume and be consumed. I was never a person who bought clothing just to take outfit photos in, with a plan then to return the clothes to the store, because I considered that unfair to the store and to the readership. Because of this practice (and folks simply returning worn clothes), some stores will actually ban people from returning items if they return too much within a certain time period. They're on to the game. I was also never going to be the person who bought clothing only to wear once, because I considered that wasteful even before I knew about the true fashion waste problem.

But I began to clock that I was buying an awful lot of clothes. I always liked clothes a lot, but my hyper-consumption began to worry me. I didn't like what was happening, but I also didn't like the urge I felt to purchase certain items of clothing because other bloggers had them, which led to more hits. Think of it like fashion clickbait. I remember a few outfits in my wardrobe that were definitely purchased because I had seen the item on someone else and thought that having said item would "elevate my style." But what was I really elevating besides my credit card debt? And the problem was the people with disposable cash could afford to buy their way into the game. They didn't need innate style if they had a deep bank account. And people wouldn't question: does that person truly have good style, or do they just come from a ton of money, privilege, and access? We love to tell everyone that if you work hard and pay your dues, good things will happen to you...but with money and privilege many skip their way straight to the head of the line in front of you, no matter how hard you've been here working all this time before they got there. People could say, "Well, that's just the way things are done," but

> "I always liked clothes a lot, but my hyper-consumption began to worry me."

26

does that actually have to be the way things are handled in our future? If so, what is the point of even trying to progress?

Back in my day, things were changing: one minute, blogging was not being taken seriously, and then suddenly one day everyone "got it," and bloggers began to sit front row at some of the most critically acclaimed fashion houses. Brands figured out how to monetize fashion blogging's growing profiles and communities. This marked the turning point, where people could follow the money.

And the brands soon began to take advantage. They monetized the bloggers by gifting them items that they would then share with their influence. This immediately drew lines between the cool kids and those who weren't considered cool enough. As usual, there's that person you've been following since the beginning and the world suddenly begins to notice their talent and it feels pretty cool, but there is also always the person who jumped into the game super-late but is now famous because they have a bigger budget and even more clothes than you. These practices began to fuel us into keeping up with one another like there was no tomorrow. We were consuming each other's consumption, and then consuming ourselves.

> "We were consuming each other's consumption, and then consuming ourselves."

Who was actually winning in this situation? When influencing and blogging first took off, brands initially didn't pay anyone. Eventually bloggers got paid, and that money bled into Instagram. But with the birth of social media came the most inexpensive marketing ever in the history of humanity for both the beauty business and the fashion industry. Before, brands would spend millions on campaigns; suddenly all they had to do (in addition to any paid marketing) was send their product to the right person...and there it was, instantly, displayed for hundreds of thousands to see daily, if the person chose to carry the bag or whatever the item was. And why wouldn't that person carry the bag? It said something about them personally that this big expensive luxury brand considered them "cool" enough to send them a little present. Even though the bloggers weren't getting paid initially, everyone was wowed by the free product being gifted. And the brands that initially paid zero for all of these sales being stoked high-fived each other as so many of us took the bait.

Gifting has actually been a longtime practice of brands and labels to editors and celebs. The gifting is part of what can make a job that doesn't pay well enough to live worth its while. That's what one magazine editor once explained to me in the midst of hauling a gigantic bag of gifted loot to a consignment store in the East Village.

Someone once said, "Comparison is the thief of joy." And social media runs off that fuel, as it drives you to consume in ways you don't need to. There are very few people who can be in spaces that focus on material possessions without weighing themselves against the person above or below them on a feed. It's part of the human condition. I realized that when gifting to bloggers began, brands were really driving a divide in the community. It catapulted some bloggers to celebrity status seemingly overnight, and mostly those who were wealthy were rewarded for being born privileged. And while, before, some of us felt compelled to buy to keep up and to feel like part of the crowd, now you had brands gifting things to the "cool people," essentially deciding with their gift who was the "in crowd." If you wanted to feel accepted, you and your uncool self, you could just go out and buy the item yourself.

Eventually I had had enough of it all, and I simply wasn't going to play this game. When brands would gift the same "in crowd" of people with the same very expensive handbag, I immediately marked that bag down as one I wouldn't even consider buying for myself, even if I liked it.

And all of this was happening side by side with countless think pieces being written about how "blogging was making the fashion industry more democratic," as if the various barriers for entry, such as being able to afford a high-quality camera or hosting a professional blog site, weren't already a hurdle for most. So much for democracy.

Social media's supposed "democratizing" effect didn't much aid race and representation. It's pretty well documented that cis white able-bodied influencers receive more sponsorship and better fees than everyone else in so many different arenas. The problem has been highlighted over and over again, to the point that multiple campaigns have been launched online to try to combat it. You only have to check out @influencerpaygap on Instagram for examples.

But it isn't just influencers who have this problem. In an appearance on *The Tamron Hall Show* in May 2021, former US *Vogue* editor-at-large André Leon Talley spoke out about finding that other (white) *Vogue* editors were being paid significantly more, saying, "And I just found out two weeks ago from someone of authority that women at *Vogue*, high, high rate fashion editors, made close to a million dollars, I never made that much in a year. I made almost $300,000, but people on the same level, maybe they were doing more work than the fashion photo shoots, were making $900,000 a year. They don't make that anymore, but this is what comes when you live in America when you're a Black person, you have to wake up and you know there's a double standard."

In addition to being paid less, Black and brown content creators are routinely held to a higher level of account by brands. The problem is so bad that now social media accounts exist where you can list your race and area of expertise and follower count, while discussing what you got paid for certain brand work. I have heard stories from more than one BIPOC friend of being offered "gifted" products from brands, only to have that brand turn around and *pay* white influencers to promote the same item. This is why we talk about inclusion riders in the influencer world. It's not enough to have a seat at the table if you're not bringing others with you. But, of course, this problem doesn't just exist in social media. It's everywhere in our society. (Even the literary world. When I decided to write this book in the summer of 2020, there was a reckoning in the publishing industry, in which writers had anonymously shared their advances, stating their race, genre, age, and publisher, using the hashtag #publishingpaidme. The discrepancies were horrifying and disheartening.)

And, of course, one of the reasons I initially shied away from working with brands on my platform is because I knew that, when it came to marginalized people, a lot of brands didn't play fair. And brands were decidedly not okay with phrases like "white supremacy" and "Black Lives Matter" until 2020, and I sure as hell wasn't going to *not* talk about these things on my platforms. So, the "pay for the play" song and dance really didn't work for what I set out to do.

Eventually I would abandon blogging altogether and give up on fashion quietly. Because it felt like yet another game where those with financial advantages swooped in and made it so no one else had a fair shot.

What I learned over the years was that I wasn't going to run in the mainstream, and I didn't want to partake in the circus of elitism that controlled and gatekept those who got into the main fashion industry and those who were left unpaid. I knew that there was a *big* problem underneath the glamour, which fed off and got more powerful from people like me not feeling "enough." There was something rotten at the heart of the industry that didn't include but, on the contrary, did exclude.

Then I zoomed out even further, and I saw my story was just a microcosm of the whole, and I mean the whole fashion industry, not just the Global North's fashion circus. The big brands were getting bigger by the minute and exploiting those at the very bottom with little pay, while also broadly selling their products to people who never felt they would fit in if they didn't consume more. They were constantly filling up a cup that could never be filled.

I kept on thinking back to the level of stuff being thrown at people who already had it, and the lack of stuff afforded to everyone else, and why it felt the people at the bottom of the consumer culture had to buy their way in or else be exploited by not being paid fairly or at all.

Fast fashion was created to exploit the people at the bottom—both the workers and the consumers. It was created to stamp out small and independent brands, often stealing directly from the Davids as it positioned itself as the Goliath. The industry would profit off the backs of those who were trapped and not those who were free. The entire industry felt morally bankrupt, and I was pretty sure I didn't fit anywhere in it.

2

COLONIZATION: THE ROOT OF THE PROBLEM

As I began to distance myself from blogging and the endless cycle of consumerism, I started to educate myself.

Now, I've tried very hard to stay in my lane here and focus on how the issue of colonialism has affected me and those I know. This book isn't meant to be an exhaustive list of *everything* in the story of colonialism. I expect to see a great many books on the subject in the future to add to an already long list. And you should read them all. But my aim here is to put things in the simplest terms and give you a little breadcrumb trail and then set you off on your journey. Because we should constantly be learning and growing. That's the reality of what all these conversations should look like. No one person is (or should be) the voice of everything.

When I looked "colonialism" up in the dictionary, it was described as "the policy or practice of acquiring full or partial political control over another country, occupying it with settlers, and exploiting it economically." According to the online dictionary Lexico.com, "colonization" is described as "the action or process of settling among and establishing control over the indigenous people of an area."

Cleopatra Tatabele, cultural educator and co-founder of the Abuela Taught Me collective, told me: "When I think about colonialism in the fashion industry...they literally are taking our resources from our lands, selling it back to us and burying garbage next to us; it's colonialism at its finest."

Let's take a moment to look at the clothing you're wearing:

Try to envision the face of the person who made the garment you're wearing:

- What color is their skin?
- How much money do they make monthly?
- No, really, like where was it made? What's it made from?
- And can you ensure that the garment worker who made it made good wages?

Now with that in mind, look at anything that's been purchased in the room you're sitting in currently. What was made locally? What wasn't? What's your socioeconomic status?

COLONIZATION IS EVERYWHERE

Have you ever wondered why English is spoken in so many different countries? It's not because the locals thought it was better. It was forcefully imposed.

Have you ever wondered why Christianity is so prevalent in so many different countries? It's because it was enforced on people as the only religion by colonizers and crusaders, to try and destroy a part of their culture and belief system and make it our own. Because ultimately that made people more governable.

- Colonization is when a country with power and resources dominates another country and proceeds to extract resources (both material and labor) while imposing new cultural norms.
- Colonization is also deeply and intrinsically linked to racism.
- Colonization is also deeply and intrinsically linked to the slave trade.
- Colonization is practically as old as humanity, but that doesn't make it right or any less devastating to the colonized. Have non-white countries colonized others? Absolutely. But when we look at colonial lines, money, and who is powerful today due to colonization, in the global scheme of wealth and resources as they're distributed, all signs point back to white supremacy.
- Colonization is, according to the Slow Factory Foundation, "based on the doctrine of cultural hierarchy and supremacy through the exploitation of land, labor and resources."
- Céline Semaan, executive director and co-founder of Slow Factory, works within a framework that focuses on three main points for colonialism: religion, fashion, and media. Now religion I'm not going to touch with a ten-foot pole, plus I have a sneaky feeling there'll be a book in the future that you can really sink your teeth in. We're going to focus on fashion and media instead, because those are the areas my work is truly about.

There's an ideology that has long been pushed that has prioritized the dominance of whiteness through "trade" and exploitation. Clothing has historically blended the differences across cultural divides. What you wear enables you to assimilate to the "dominant" culture. That means that if you live in a country that was colonized, blending in was historically sometimes a means of survival, because resistance was often met with, well...death.

But it's not just clothing that can be weaponized in a system built off colonialism.

It's food.

It's land.

It's hair.

It's body hair.

It's spirituality.

It's sexuality.

Our society is so threatened by the conversation about deconstructing colonialism that people take great pains to hide the truth. What we really need to do is look at all these systems that we operate within and reform them, figuring out what restorative justice should be in light of it all and the sharing of power, money, and resources. And I'll tell you...a lot of folks don't really want to see that happen. The *Guardian* reported in April 2012 that attempts had been made to rewrite history by destroying evidence of some of the most shameful acts and crimes committed during the final years of the British Empire, including records of abuse, torture, and sometimes murder of Mau Mau insurgents by British colonial authorities, and the alleged massacre of unarmed villagers in Malaya by soldiers of the Scots Guard, in order to prevent these documents from "embarrassing" the post-independence government.

But Britain isn't the only one shamelessly trying to hide a past of exploitation and harm done to marginalized communities and minorities. On January 21, 2021, on NBC News, Robyn Autry noted that "[Donald] Trump's '1776 Report' was compiled by an eighteen-person commission of mostly male conservative educators (no historians), who assembled the document and released it on Martin Luther King Jr. Day. In just forty pages (twenty of which are appendices), the report offered a framework for a 'patriotic education' to counter 'false and fashionable' histories that paint the country's founders as hypocrites who espoused egalitarian principles while protecting the institution of slavery."

So much of the information we learn about the systems of governance is provided by those who hold the most power. When I think back to what was taught to me as a child (in the eighties and nineties), "colonialism" wasn't exactly the name that was given in the US. Instead, we learned of brave and daring "explorers," which sounds way more dignified than "thieves" and "oppressors," right? There was no focus in curriculum about the harm these explorers brought to the good folks who already lived in the lands that were conquered. See: Thanksgiving. The focus was *always* on the victors and the "good" things that came out of the bloodbaths. I mean, in school we actually were forced to sing songs about Christopher Columbus.

"In 1492 Columbus sailed the ocean blue! Christopher Columbus, Christopher Columbus, Christopher Columbus, he was our man!" It's enough to make me want to lose my lunch. Are they still teaching children this crap? Quick scan of YouTube says yes.

Christopher Columbus was a rapist and a murderer. And I do not say that lightly. On October 12, 2015, Michael Coard wrote in an article titled "This Is the Monster Celebrated on Columbus Day" in *Philadelphia* magazine: "Imagine that a man who tortured, raped and murdered innocent people and then robbed them of their homes is worshiped each year as a hero."

Was America built off slavery and oppression? Why, yes, it was. Are there still systemic barriers within America that keep marginalized people from advancing in certain ways? Why, yes, there are.

TRADITIONALLY PILLAGED COUNTRIES

The notion that someone automatically wants and needs something that you have thoroughly used is wrapped up in the narrative of white saviorism. Let's break down why I say "traditionally pillaged," instead of "developing countries" or "third world." First and foremost, "third world" has become a very offensive term. According to Investopedia.com: "Third World countries included nations in Asia and Africa that were not aligned with either the United States or the Soviet Union. Now, in part because the Soviet Union no longer exists, the definition of Third World is outdated and considered offensive." So, there's that. But what about "developing countries"? That one's another doozy of a phrase. The countries that are being referred to are resource-rich and labor-rich.

Let's look at the output of countries that are often considered "developing." Every country in the continent of Africa has a resource that is considered highly profitable in the Global North: Benin cotton. Mali cotton. Togo, cotton as well. The reason the Gold Coast was called the Gold Coast is because it had gold! Still don't believe me? Okay, here goes: Morocco has textiles and produces clothes. Algeria has petroleum and natural gas.

Libya has crude oil. Sudan has gold. Chad: oil. Kenya: tea. Ethiopia: coffee. Democratic Republic of the Congo: diamonds. Zambia: coffee. Namibia: diamonds. Botswana: diamonds. Mozambique has aluminum. Sierra Leone produces rubber. The Ivory Coast: cocoa beans. Zimbabwe: platinum.

Actually, let's break it down. Since I consider both the United Kingdom and the United States "home," let's look at both countries and some of the countries in the Global South they've colonized or ruled over in the past and what these countries export.

The Bahamas' main exports include mineral products and salt, animal products, rum, chemicals, fruit, and vegetables. The Bahamas' biggest export partner is the United States.

Barbados's main exports include manufactures, sugar, molasses, rum, other foodstuffs and beverages, chemicals, and electrical components. Barbados's biggest export partner is the United States.

Belize's main exports include sugar, bananas, citrus, clothing, fish products, molasses, wood, and crude oil. Belize's biggest export partner is the United Kingdom, followed by the United States.

Botswana's main exports include diamonds, copper, nickel, soda ash, beef, and textiles. Botswana's biggest export partner is Belgium.

Egypt's main exports include natural gas and non-petroleum products such as ready-made clothes, cotton textiles, medical and petrochemical products, citrus fruits, rice, and dried onion, and more recently cement, steel, and ceramics. Egypt's biggest export partner is the United Arab Emirates (a former protectorate of the United Kingdom).

Fiji's main exports include sugar, garments, gold, timber, fish, molasses, mineral water, and coconut oil. Fiji's main export partners are the United Kingdom and the United States.

Ghana's main exports include oil, gold, cocoa, timber, tuna, bauxite, aluminum, manganese ore, diamonds, and horticultural products. Ghana's main export partner is India, a former colony of the United Kingdom.

India's main exports include oil and minerals, precious stones and metals, cotton, and rice. Like basmati rice? Thank you, India (and Pakistan)!

Iraq...oil. That didn't surprise you. The oil goes everywhere but mostly to India and China, which export to everywhere else. Look around the room you're currently sitting in. Something within your line of sight has been produced and manufactured in India or China.

Jamaica's main exports include aluminum and bauxite (which account for approximately one-third of export earnings); sugar, bananas, coffee and other agricultural products, beverages and tobacco, and chemicals constitute most of the remainder. Jamaica's main export partner is the United States.

Nigeria's main exports include crude oil and petroleum.

Pakistan's main export is cotton.

South Africa's main exports include corn, diamonds, fruits, gold, metals and minerals, sugar, and wool. South Africa's biggest export partners include China, Germany, and the United States.

Sri Lanka's main exports include textiles and apparel, tea and spices, electronics, rubber manufactures, fish, and precious stones. Sri Lanka's biggest export partners are the European Union and the United States.

Chances are you've eaten something this week that was grown in one of the countries listed above. Chances are the clothing you're wearing had something to do with the countries listed above (check your label now). Chances are you've purchased something MADE IN INDIA, MADE IN BANGLADESH in recent times.

My point is, there are so many nations that are resource-rich. So why are these countries still considered "developing"? Why aren't they fully developed? Could it be because there's been a lot of pillaging and thieving going on throughout the history of colonization, much to the detriment of these countries' economies?

Is it true to say that newly independent nations had to rebuild from scratch, and to do so many had to take on massive debt, which left their economies fragile and open to exploitation? Plus, is it fair to say that the terms for what is regarded as "valuable" are set by the Global North, which means colonized nations may have given/sold access to resources more freely than they would have, had they known the perceived value? It can't just be because the people who live in these countries aren't good at business. *I think, friends, it's the colonization.*

Centuries of pillaging affect where your country falls on the global scale and determine factors such as wealth and infrastructures like education. We need to teach the truth about colonialism in our curricula, and we also need to look back at history and revise it—no longer passing on the one-sided education provided to us by those in power, but acknowledging the fuller picture of what happened, which includes looking from the standpoint of those who didn't previously get to be a part of history.

Colonialism: A Roundtable Discussion

In order to get that fuller picture, I asked some friends about it. Think of this as a roundtable discussion, because it takes more than one person to tell any part of this story. All of the people around this table are marginalized people who are either educators or work within the fashion industry in some capacity. I wanted their stories particularly as they pertain to colonialism.

CLEOPATRA TATABELE is Black and Taíno (the Taíno are the Indigenous people of the Caribbean and Florida; colonialism began for them as early as the late fifteenth century): "Taíno people are the *first* people to be colonized and also the longest amount of time that we've had to be colonized since Columbus came on our island...This colonization is still taking place today. Not only are we being taken advantage of by all these huge companies that are telling us "hey, you get fifty percent off if you spend ten dollars," and then we get all these clothes and then, at the end of all that, it gets thrown out in the garbage. Our lands are filled with landfills. So, when I think about where our trash goes, it also goes into the communities, and the landfills are also in the communities that are the poorest and also Black or Indigenous."

SWATEE DEEPAK, feminist activist and co-founder of the *Remember Who Made Them* podcast and campaign, gave me a very succinct history of how colonialism came to be in India, when I asked about the history: "When the British East India Company set sail for India [in 1608], its sole purpose was to disrupt and unseat the Indian textile trade and market, which was the strongest, biggest, and most profitable in the world at the time. The East India Company went on to be the gateway company to British colonial rule, exploiting my community and ancestors, and extracting and destabilizing the natural resources in the region. It's well documented how much Britain plundered from India, which before British colonialization was one of the richest countries in the world, and when the British left it was one of the poorest. Britain took an estimated $45 trillion from India over 173 years of colonial rule...When India finally gained freedom and independence from the British in 1947, due to a plethora of political reasons and fragmentation of ideologies, it was 'partitioned' by the British into what is modern-day India, Pakistan, and Bangladesh. The partition was drawn on religious lines, and all my grandparents found themselves on the wrong side. My grandparents all had to rebuild their lives as refugees in India, and my parents left India as immigrants to come to the UK to give their children a better future."

In 2014, Ian Jack in the *Guardian* reported, "For at least two centuries the handloom weavers of Bengal produced some of the world's most desirable fabrics, especially the fine muslins, light as 'woven air,' that were in such demand for dressmaking and so cheap that Britain's own cloth manufacturers conspired to cut off the fingers of Bengali weavers and break their looms."

And in 2019 Nitin Singh and Nikhil Venkatesa wrote in a story on the website of Indian fashion label SGBG Atelier: "The [East India] Company didn't just focus on crippling Indian handlooms and weavers in the short term with their price fixing strategy and enforcing it through violence; they also adopted long-term taxation strategies to ensure that the Indian textile trade would be permanently crippled."

AJA BARBER: "Britain has a long history of meddling in thriving economies for profit. The notion that any company that claims the jobs it brings overseas is an altruistic move really should be codified 'it is cheaper.'"

CÉLINE SEMAAN, of the Slow Factory Foundation, has looked at how colonialism harmed Lebanon: "Lebanon has been colonized by dozens of empires and nations throughout history. This has shaped our identity, how we relate to culture and politics, as well as how we dress, talk and exist within today's colonial landscape...I recently learned that, under the rule of the Ottoman Empire in Lebanon in the 1800s, women in my country were responsible for harvesting natural silk to export to Europe, particularly Lyon, for the ruling class in France to enjoy fine silk. What was fascinating was to find out that the working conditions of the women in my country were very similar to today's silk production, which is to live close to the poverty line and to work long hours with very little pay...[In addition,] the women working the silk trade in Lebanon were forced to dedicate land space for mulberry trees alone: paired with the consequences on trade during the First World War, the situation left them and their communities to face the Great Famine that Lebanon was under [from 1915 to 1918]."

DOMINIQUE DRAKEFORD, thought leader and sustainability entrepreneur, on Black American identity and colonialism: "I think the history of the fashion/slave trade as it leads to the cotton boom and industrial revolution is a more well-known historical timestamp, as it relates to the creation of the fashion industry and our current capitalist society as a whole...[But] in West Africa, indigo was an economic and spiritual currency across fashion, beauty, and wellness. It had many cosmetic, medicinal, and spiritual uses, but West African women, in particular, were master dyers and traders, using their indigo wealth throughout ancient empires. Indigo clothing was the largest commodity sold and traded on the West African coast. However, it was a cornerstone of the transatlantic slave trade—one of the hidden commodities that fueled the European colonial empires. Africans were sought particularly for their agricultural skills in rice, sugar, cotton, but also their advanced skills in textiles, including cultivation of indigo plantations in America, the Caribbean, and South America, which used the expertise (forced labor) of Africans who were the sustainability experts of both agriculture and textiles."

AJA BARBER: "In school we learn about cotton planting and the slave trade (ironically enough, slavery aside, my family still has connections to cotton production, as one of my uncles used to work for a company that processed cotton fibers used in tampons), but we don't usually take a moment to connect those acts to the way we consume today, and we don't look at slavery as a foundational building block of all these systems. The narrative of slavery shows Black people as enslaved people and those who were 'conquered' and 'sold.' It doesn't show us as stewards of the land we tended through slavery. It doesn't portray us as environmentalists."

A NOTE ON OPPRESSION IN AMERICA

Early expedition parties from European countries explored the world and brought settlers to what is today the United States of America. With those settlers, they brought colonized people from various African nations to serve as slaves, who arguably built the country all unpaid and while suffering nothing but trauma and endless abuse. That trauma still shows up through our culture today.

While enslaving people from Africa, those settlers constantly and consistently aided in stamping out the population of Indigenous people who already lived in what is today the United States. Those settlers took their land, brought diseases (smallpox blankets, anyone?), and killed off entire populations through cruel measures. Ever seen that famous black-and-white photo of the man standing next to an absolute mountain of bison skulls? That photo is dark because it represents an active move by white settlers to hunt all the bison, which was an important food source for Indigenous people. If you take away a food source from a group of people, that is active genocide. (Similar to polluting waterways.) Because of moves like that, the American bison nearly became extinct. And today the North American Indigenous people suffer greatly from the atrocities of the past that have harmed them.

There is something so deeply violent and heartbreaking about stripping a group of people of their culture. Taking their children away and putting them in boarding schools, so that the youth have no connection to their culture. That's a systemic stamping out of a group of people. And that is exactly what happened to North American Indigenous people. As Mary Annette Pember explained in The Atlantic *in 2019: "This is what achieving civilization looked like in practice: Students were stripped of all things associated with Native life. Their long hair, a source of pride for many Native* peoples, was cut short, usually into identical bowl hair-cuts. They exchanged traditional clothing for uniforms and embarked on a life influenced by strict military-style regi-mentation. Students were physically punished for speaking their Native languages. Contact with family and community members was discouraged or forbidden altogether."

Another article by Nandi Howard published in Bitch magazine in 2020 notes that "According to the National Park Service, 'Clothing was also used to reinforce social distinctions among enslaved Africans and between the masters and their slaves.' A digital archive for Mount Vernon, George Washington's Virginia plantation, details Washington's clothing expectations for the people he and his wife enslaved. He wanted them to wear linen due to the cheap price of the cloth; he also required his slaves to create their own clothing to further cut costs."

So we're clear: enslaved people brought from one country to another are thereupon subjected to rules that require dress codes, all so that two hundred years later many mostly white-owned businesses can mimic those dress codes and make a bundle. Yikes.

Politician and environmentalist Heather McTeer Toney wrote in All We Can Save: "Black folks have always had a deep and physical connection to the environment. The land that our ancestors were forced to work was the very same space where they lived. The field where our mothers toiled was often the place where they also gave birth. Our his-tory has entwined us with the land in a profound way, and *our connection to the land is as symbiotic as bees to flowers. Yet our voices are constantly ignored on matters concerning climate impacts and environmental protections."*

AJA BARBER: "How does colonialism show up today?"

SWATEE DEEPAK: "Fashion's colonialism problem isn't just what we see on social media, in the stores, in magazines, or on the runways; it's present in the trade policies and agreements that are hidden in plain sight...And on the link between the fashion industry and racism: it's not just about exploitation of BIPOC bodies and minds, but also that fashion corporations are not afraid to use the force of the state and to support police brutality in intimidation of labor organizers and workers. When we speak to garment workers' collectives and unions around the world, including India, it's highlighted to us how so many movements around the world feel solidarity with the Black Lives Matter protests, because they totally understand what police brutality feels like (and other forms of systemic racism)."

AJA BARBER: "The accuracy there hurts, and that's also why I got so irate to see so many brands on the #PayUp list throwing black squares up on their social media account. I wholeheartedly do not seek the support in any movement I participate in from groups that oppress other marginalized people if given an opportunity. That's not the support that we seek or need. Our liberation cannot be built off of the oppression of others."

KALKIDAN LEGESSE, MBA, founder of sustainable resale platform Shwap and ethical marketplace Sancho's Shop: "The fashion industry as we know it today was birthed out of the promise of cheaper labor costs in the Global East. As wages increased in countries like the UK, emergent brands saw an opportunity to create products at lower cost elsewhere. Companies learned that they could keep prices down using a number of tactics, including the weakening of garment worker rights, prolonged suppression of pay, short-term contracts with suppliers to create internal price wars, and more."

AJA BARBER: "So, let's be clear about another thing. Often, I see brands make the case that working with suppliers in the ways in which they do gives freedom to the supplier...because they wouldn't want to interfere with the workings of that group of people and how they do business, would they? Hmmm. Sounds good on paper but, if we're honest, if you already know that you hold a lot of power in that situation, then you can paint a pretty picture while never acknowledging that you set the terms of everything in that deal."

KALKIDAN LEGESSE: "For me, the link to colonization is the confidence with which the fashion industry did this, while also telling the tale that this is the best possible outcome for developing countries. That the best they could hope for is the opportunity to work underpaid in unsafe factories so that owners in the West could become wealthier. That is the ideological dominance of Europe and the West. It's only now that the academics, activists, policy makers, and the business owners in the West are considering the link between the extractive business model and climate change, and leaning heavily on Indigenous teachings to do so, that this model seems absurd."

AJA BARBER: "The concept of white saviorism and 'it's a good job in that country,' and just the concept that these countries would absolutely fail without interference from the West is pretty toxic. But no one wants to acknowledge that this cycle is never about altruism or 'bringing jobs to people.' It's about stopping change happening from within."

KALKIDAN LEGESSE: "The ability to move continents to continue to sell fast fashion sends a clear and firm message to garment workers, factory owners, and policy makers. Their work is either extractive and for the financial gain of the brand owners, or it is dispensable. Colonization treats people and places as inputs into a model designed to make a small number of people very wealthy."

CÉLINE SEMAAN: "All the 'leverage' of global markets, from cheap labor and resources to 'unskilled' manufacturing expertise, are rooted in inequalities that were created in the emergence of the colonial era over the past few hundred years."

ANYANGO MPINGA, Nairobi-born eco-innovator and social activist: "Fashion has a history of exploiting the crafts of Indigenous cultures, misusing members of marginalized communities for cheap labor, and also pushing a system of presenting collections that are mostly accessible to elite groups of people, when in actual fact it doesn't take much to be inclusive."

"Following the trade routes of the fashion industry's basic resources, like cotton, silk, polyester, manufacturing, and labor, we can trace all the trajectory back to source with the multiple import/export back-and-forth between the many countries entrenched with fast fashion production: these trade routes map identically with historical colonial routes."

AJA BARBER: "Let's do a quick exercise. Tell me a designer off the top of your head from the entire continent of Africa. You've got fifty-four countries to pick from, and a whole lot of talent to pick from. But I suspect you're finding it a bit challenging, aren't you? I'm not judging you for that, because the entire system mostly praises European and American designers, with a handful of Asian designers thrown in for good measure."

ANYANGO MPINGA: "We still see brands thriving on the oppression of workers and marginalized communities. Africa is still a dumping ground for the rejects of the fast fashion industry. The fashion industry still gives preferential treatment toward designers from certain fashion institutions; and even within those schools, there's little diversity in the faculty and even the student community...We still have retailers that aren't selling enough products from African creatives and, when they do, it's through pop-ups showcasing designers from Africa with short-term relationships, rather than forming the long-term retail relationships afforded to European or American designers. Unfortunately, this still sends a message to members of certain communities that they don't quite belong in certain spaces and their presence isn't valued...I've heard designers talk about how the only way they're going to get their designs seen on a global stage is to be featured by one of the big multi-brand luxury retailers. But it's a long and winding road to get there."

DOMINIQUE DRAKEFORD: "Nearly all multi-million/billion-dollar global brands have adopted principles and practices of slave-based labor primarily toward skilled BIPOC women throughout their supply chain to generate wealth and continue an ecosystem of exploitation. Additionally, it's important to understand that these are the same brands that acquired their 'generational wealth' from a long history of Black slave labor pointing back to indigo and cotton."

AJA BARBER: "How do we do away with these systems and move forward into a more equitable fashion landscape, where there are more seats at the table for everyone? The answer I have for you is a multi-leveled one: there's more than one way to get from point A to point B and, as we've never solved this problem in our modern time, no one really has one true answer. The thing I think about most, however, is power. Who has it, and how do we redistribute it? What does that even look like?"

SWATEE DEEPAK: "If workers were more represented, we would also see a massive change in gender inequality, since eighty percent of garment workers are women. If women workers were able to represent their communities in leadership positions or at decision-making tables, you can expect that there will be better working conditions—less sexual violence and harassment in the workplace, better parental leave and childcare policies, better job security, and more. All of this benefits people of all genders... Those in power (cis white men, and others who benefit from capitalist-patriarchal colonialism) *absolutely* need to change and give up power... And we need to stop the system of wealth accumulation. The global apparel market is valued at three trillion dollars, 3,000 billion, and accounts for two percent of the world's gross domestic product (per research by Fashion United). Shouldn't workers who create the means for such vast profits be able to live life with dignity? Aren't there enough profits to go round?"

KALKIDAN LEGESSE: "To challenge the former we need to, as a global society, better allocate value gained and costs experienced equally. This means dealing with waste effectively and assigning the environmental cost of waste not to the unlucky people who live closest to polluted areas but to the organizations whose business models create the waste and earn them taxable profits."

AJA BARBER: "Wealth redistribution for this system is the future we both want to live in, Kalkidan. It should be the system that we all want to live in, especially if we believe in being antiracist and in an equity-driven future."

KALKIDAN LEGESSE: "To challenge the latter we need to embrace an increase in the Global South's minimum acceptable wage. This means doing away with fashion billionaires, whose fortunes could transform the lived experiences of millions of garment workers. It means brands should look at reinvesting their earnings into the communities that make their clothes, and allowing those communities an independence and future not directly tied to the brand's performance. It means buying from Black and brown folk."

AJA BARBER: "Hear, hear!"

ANYANGO MPINGA: "If each of us made a decision to take just one positive action to support the growth of one artisan, worker, or designer from a marginalized community, we would transform the industry as we know it."

AJA BARBER: "So, here's the thing: I've always believed that the only way we can really democratize the playing field is by spreading our money around. We're not going to buy our way out of this mess, of course...but if you want a more even fashion landscape, that looks like thinking about where your money flows and making sure it doesn't all flow in one specific direction. On my platform I really focus on highlighting brands from the Global South as I see them. There are designers and artisans in all the countries where our clothing is made (of course there are...

how else does clothing get made?). Instead of using a middle person from a wealthier country to get the goods into our hands, I'd rather give my money directly to that person and highlight and amplify their work. All these monopolies aren't really that good for us. If I give some money directly to those on the ground and get a product directly from them, in a small way, that changes the direction things are going. If a lot of us are doing that and thinking about those purchases, there's bound to be a small shift."

CÉLINE SEMAAN: "Colonialism is at its root a question of exploiting across geographies. Its roots are in setting up colonies to extract resources and labor. Therefore, the move away from colonial systems is toward a more local, symbiotic, and egalitarian system, in any way possible."

DOMINIQUE DRAKEFORD: "The pillars of the system, which I've coined as public policy, marketing, and education, all have to be strategically ripped from the roots." Now obviously that's a huge undertaking that's going to take years of undoing. Abolishing something that has been hundreds of years in the making can't happen overnight, so Drakeford offers a more short-term solution. "I believe we have to focus on creating adjacent alternative systems, institutions, and infrastructures, collectively run and operated by BIPOC communities."

KIMBERLY JENKINS, groundbreaking educator and founder of fashionandrace.org, offers a few steps to get us there: "There are three suggested ways to do away with colonial systems:

1. Divest from parts of the industry, electing to spend your income and resources within systems that contribute in meaningful ways to your community and culture.

2. If divesting is not feasible, do your best to educate yourself on the ways that the tentacles of colonialism influence your life—this can be done by following people and/organizations 'doing the work,' and perhaps you can donate toward their efforts.
3. Communicate, making your voice heard and grievances known to actors in the industry who uphold the status quo and perpetuate oppressive, colonialist systems in the fashion industry—for example, this can take the shape of demanding more diverse products, calling out harmful or insulting images and misappropriated objects, and demanding fair labor rights for garment workers."

There are so many ways forward, and we're just getting started. But, in the apt words of Dr. Ayana Elizabeth Johnson, "Everyone find your place."

POSTCOLONIALISM AND THE LEGACY

Nowadays, colonialism shows up all over our planet, especially in the places where our products are manufactured, but also in the places our trash goes and our used clothing gets dumped.

Where do your clothes go when you're tired of them? Once you bag them up and give them to charity? Well, about 10 to 20 percent of the clothing donated gets sold. A few charities are doing really good work trying to mitigate the large amount of fast fashion they receive, but for the most part...very few are selling every piece they receive. Instead, it gets sorted and some-times it goes to a different charity, but very often the clothing that doesn't make the cut gets turned into a bale and shipped to various locations in the Global South. But we are going to focus on Accra, Ghana, because Accra is home to Kantamanto Market, which is probably the world's largest secondhand market. So, what does this market look like? Kantamanto receives 15 million garments a week. Which is surprisingly the same number of Americans who were estimated to have suffered from a spending addiction, according to the American Psychological Association in 2011. (That irony isn't lost on me, either.)

Kantamanto is a thriving hub, and probably one of the most buzzing places on Earth. Both vendors and customers arrive sometimes before the crack of dawn. The big day for the market is Thursday (and it starts *very* early in the morning). That's when a hundred importers—mainly from Europe, the US, and Canada, but even Asia, especially Korea and China—unload containers to sell their bales to retailers. The atmosphere becomes frenetic, with kayayei (women porters who do backbreaking work) zipping up and down the market with bales upon bales of clothes that will soon be opened and ready for sale. Each bale is about three feet by two feet in size, wrapped and tied with plastic string. These distributors are selling the clothes in bulk packages to local vendors, who in turn sell them to their customers. It's on Wednesdays and Saturdays that the retail begins, with 30,000 traders laying out the purchased goods that are sellable (not all bales are created equal, and it's a total gamble as to what will be discovered in each bale before it's bought and opened).

Due to the gambling nature of bale buying, there's a lot of debt for sellers of Kantamanto. "Less than twenty percent of the retailers in Kantamanto make an actual net profit on the average bale, and retailers of female clothes are even less likely to make a profit," says Liz Ricketts, from the OR Foundation, who are integral to all research in this book about Kantamanto (all facts presented here can be accessed through the OR Foundation's work). Many retailers have to turn to taking on debt in order to set up their shop, which costs around two Ghanaian cedis per month (34 cents), and often those loans come with an incredibly high interest rate of more than 30 percent. So, most of these traders are already in debt before they begin work. "Many retailers take out a loan from one bank to pay off a loan from another in a revolving cycle of debt from which they are unlikely to escape," Liz adds. "Enormous amounts of cash circulate through the market, and many retailers are able to take home enough money to cover at least some of their basic expenses, but it's not uncommon for retailers to have to choose between paying for electricity, water or their children's school fees."

But why is it so hard to make a profit? The answer: fast fashion.

The quality of clothing has declined, and although the early buyers who generally start trawling the markets at five-thirty A.M. can get branded goods, the rest of the clothing is mostly low-quality fast fashion. The bale-buying business is a gigantic risk because the traders are dealing in highly depreciating assets. Some strike it lucky and get a bale full of high-quality goods that can be sold on at a good price...but that's a very small number. For all the sellers, however, it's a risk they're willing to take, because the options outside of the market are currently few.

This is where a lot of those purchases we probably didn't need end up, and it is these people who have to sift through your bad decision-making to try to find a way of making a living out of the abundance of low-value stuff you packed off to the charity shop. "The pace of the market mirrors the pace of fast fashion production and retail in the Global North," Liz explains. "Kantamanto retailers are 'restocking' new styles twice a week. This also means that any garments that cannot be sold typically leave the market as waste only one to two weeks after being unloaded in Kantamanto. This is especially mind-boggling when you consider the long and winding path (and carbon footprint) these garments take to get to Kantamanto."

The things that we think we're giving away and being "do gooders" by doing so are simply becoming someone else's problem. We really need to weigh the impact of an action or system over the intention. Intention doesn't matter when there's harm being done.

What happens to the clothing that still doesn't get sold? Forty percent of clothes that don't end up getting sold or repurposed in Kantamanto become waste and are taken to landfill, informal dumping grounds, or burn piles, or are put in the sea. As it turns out, Kantamanto Market is the single largest consolidated source of solid waste in the city of Accra. But, more important still, it costs the city of Accra money to mitigate the waste that comes from the world's dumped clothing. "That means the municipal government of Accra spends over a hundred thousand dollars every year on tipping fees alone for secondhand clothing waste at landfill; that doesn't include the diesel for trucks, maintenance, and labor. Nor does it include the fact that in 2019 secondhand clothing caused Accra's main engineered landfill to catch fire," says Liz.

Just imagine if the world kept dumping clothing on *your* doorstep and your tax money was used to clean it up. You'd be pissed, as would I. "The government of Ghana has taken on debt to carry the cost of disposal for other countries' waste clothing," Liz says. It's bad for the government, and it's bad for the people. Old Fadama is where a lot of the unsold clothing from Accra ends up; it's home to 80,000 people, and it's built on top of dumped clothing. These people are becoming physically displaced by the clothing that is disenfranchising their way of life.

All this clothing has become both a humanitarian and environmental crisis. And although we can work toward a circular economy in the Global North all we want, if the actions we take to get there foster fast fashion behaviors in the Global South, then we have made absolutely no progress. This is why sustainability advocates in the Global North must stop treating Africa as an afterthought and treat it as a first thought. The scale at which things are being produced will *always* be a problem. Now consider whether you have the intention of giving whatever item you are looking at buying a long and fruitful life.

Meanwhile, you may be wondering what one of the world's largest secondhand markets has to do with colonialism. Here's where it gets murky. A report by Victoria Okoye featured in The Style Idle in 2014 noted that photographer Nana Kofi Acquah, in his writings on Kantamanto, says that "locally, when the importation of used clothes, cars, and other items began in the sixties and seventies, it was called *broni we wu* ('the white person has died'), built around the conception that no one in their right mind would willingly give away such nice articles, so the people must have died, and that's how they arrived in Ghana."

And why might our old possessions have been regarded as "nice"? "Under colonial rule Ghanaians were expected to conform to Western notions of professionalism, including in the way they dressed," Liz explains. "Wearing Western-style clothing began to signal proximity to power, and the media also played a role in dictating what was appropriate or not. This meant that when secondhand clothing began pouring into Ghana (post-independence) from the Global North there was a market ready to receive it, not because citizens did not have clothing, but because wearing foreign clothing became a tool for visually crossing class barriers and for navigating the oppressive legacy of colonialism."

So, the demand for this type of clothing came from a system of colonialism where style of dress could get you further. "The secondhand clothing trade reinforced a cycle of exploitation and dependency, which ultimately perpetuates colonial power dynamics. Secondhand clothing has decimated the local fashion industry, not only by destroying local textile production but by making it impossible for emerging designers to compete with the cheap secondhand goods," says Liz.

And here's the thing: although colonialism may not exist today exactly as it did centuries back, legacies of that time persist in interfering with global value systems. Chloe Asaam, a womens-wear designer and community organizer, who also works with the OR Foundation, sees it "in terms of altering the way we, as a people, appreciated what was ours. This legacy shows up and per-severes in the little validity or worth given to (ourselves included) things from and made here. Our craftsmanship, the precision, time and thought it takes—and appreciation it deserves—have diminished over the years."

Which essentially has resulted in Ghanaians valuing their own craftsmanship as lesser than the secondhand clothing flowing into their country, because the system of what is valued and what is not has been bankrupted by the notion of power and white supremacy. Chloe explains that "by virtue of being made and shipped from overseas, it is automatically deemed as superior, it is seen as better—a mindset that stems from colonialism. And with the masses preferring stuff/products from the Global North to those produced in the region, it is very difficult for 'Made in Ghana' products to thrive."

And the faster our fashion markets move the faster others want to move as well. A few short years ago people were praising the speed at which some chains could get a dress copied directly from the runway and into stores. But this cycle doesn't just harm everyone within the supply chain, it harms those at the end of the supply chain as well.

> "This cycle doesn't just harm everyone within the supply chain, it harms those at the end of the supply chain as well."

This fast fashion perpetuates urgency, detachment, and indifference toward clothing, basically marketing clothing as disposable, which Chloe explains is "a concept essentially foreign to Ghanaian culture where clothing is heritage, where clothing is shared, borrowed, and passed down among siblings/family. Most especially when it comes to native, traditional, and celebratory clothing."

The shift away from treasuring and valuing clothing is harming us all. Our culture, our ethos, our way of life. Who are the best upcyclers of clothing on the planet? I believe it is the people in Kantamanto.

Kantamanto is a perfect example of sustainability as an integral part of culture. Within the market you can find cobblers and seamstresses. There are dyers, screen-printers, and places to buy trimming. If your garment isn't perfect, you can leave the market with a garment that has been tailored to your needs. These sorts of ideas should be implemented in secondhand markets around the world. It's this make-do-and-mend ethos that makes the Ghanaian customer an active part of fashion sustainability.

Many tend to think in the Global North that when something happens here, like the "sustainability" movement, it's "new" and we're reinventing the wheel, y'all. Hold us back! But if we stopped being myopic, we could find solutions in people who are creating sustainability at the end of our supply chain.

With recent moves toward "sustainable fashion" and "circular supply chains," certain big brands do have their eyes on Kantamanto, but in the wrong way. Again, per Liz, "Big Fashion sees Kantamanto as an extraction site." Who saw this coming? (Raises hand.) Obviously while Kantamanto is doing an amazing job of upcycling the clothing waste of the world, what do I hate more than greenwashing? Saviorism used as a marketing tool to further line your own pockets, while still not really cleaning up your mess or changing the system in which you operate.

"That system is one of extracting raw resources under conditions of exploitation to transform through consolidated technology into a value-added product and then centralize the financial gains to be made back into the hands of mostly white men. For the companies operating in this type of economy, whether they call it linear or circular, the goal remains to source as much material as possible for the lowest internalized cost. In this system Kantamanto is a colonial extraction site," says Liz. (Phew, she went full sustainable fashion mode...it even tripped up my editor decoder. "Circular" means create and recreate and recreate, and "linear" means create and dispose.)

Essentially, these big companies want to come to Kantamanto, take the waste that is polluting neighborhoods for next to nothing, put it into a blender to melt the materials down into new materials (this is a very simplified definition...no one @ me). They want to make new items out of the old waste, while claiming they're taking it off the hands of the sellers, when in actuality they should pay a hefty price for it because it shouldn't be polluting *anyone on this planet's* neighborhood.

And, yes, it is better for the planet, but also a great opportunity for brands to profit over and over again from a problem they've created. The goal is always to source as cheaply as possible, which often means making a good profit off of someone else's labor.

Certain "sustainable" fast fashion brands are actively looking to help take some of the waste from these secondhand markets in order to make new clothing with it, but they are extracting it for next to nothing (leaving those traders within the market operating at a loss)—all the while patting themselves on the back for helping "those poor Africans." Doesn't this sound familiar? Like the concept of taking from poorer countries but not sharing the profits or the resources? This is the business model of colonialism at play. As Liz puts it: "The global secondhand trade is part of the colonial business model, where the corporate entity is the colonizer and everyone else is the colony." So these "raw resources are extracted from the colony, sent to the colonizer for value to be added by patented technological processing, then exported back to colonies to consume and, in doing so, to pay money back to the colonizer."

None of us should be thanking any brand that participates in recycling clothes or puts out those handy bins for you to throw away your own clothing waste in their stores. They *should* be doing that (and not using it as an enticement for you to buy more), and they shouldn't be using it in their marketing material to make you feel good about their actions.

Their development and funding of this sustainability technology is really just another business model because, as Liz says, "Fashion companies want to take the clothes that are waste, the clothes that they produced in the first place, have people in Ghana sort them for essentially no minimum wage, and then turn the clothes into new materials for the circular economy to sell back to Ghanaians and into other markets all over the world."

The fashion companies are interested in the "solution," but only if it once again adds to their profit margins. And although there is an argument that they are attempting to clean up the mess, there has been no decided shift in power and who holds it. The questions you have to ask are: Does this decentralize the wealth in this system? Will this end the exploitation of folks in that region? Hardly. This is once again a circular model of exploitation, because people from Ghana were trafficked as slaves and sent to the Americas to tend to the cotton fields, which is part of the heart of centuries of oppression and violence. (Exhale.)

Kantamanto's waste stream has been called a "gold mine." For centuries gold and human beings have been the major raw resources extracted from West Africa. Under British rule Ghana was called the Gold Coast. For more than two hundred years Ghana's coast was where slave traders landed their ships to take their captive human cargo aboard. The next wave of extraction feels uncomfortable, to say the least.

All of this is connected. This cycle doesn't end until we have a shift in power, because as long as marginalized people are constantly looked at as resources and afterthoughts, there will always be loopholes for exploitation. Here's what I think should be happening in Kantamanto:

1. Work with those in the ecosystem.
2. Pay them those Global North wages to help mitigate this mess.
3. Employ the upcyclers and designers of Kantamanto within your own supply chain to teach you how to design better and how to upcycle the garments.
4. *Stop* slashing and burning.
5. Short of this, take your hand and dig out your wallet. Take out your checkbook. Now write a big juicy no-strings-attached check.

No one's looking for you to further invest your profit into a mess that you've created and profited from. No one needs that.

"We cannot allow circularity to end up as another green-washer marketing ploy," says Liz. "We must learn from the perspectives and the voices traditionally disenfranchised. The titans of the linear economy must step aside."

We will never get out of this mess by allowing those who caused the problem to take ownership and profit from the solution.

3

GLOBAL WEALTH: WHO'S HARMING WHO?

'**ve heard it.

You've heard it.

We've all heard it.

"I shop fast fashion because I'm poor."

But do you challenge the descriptor of "poor" as probably ill-fitting?

Because being broke is a state; poverty is systemic.

Let's face it, no one wants to be poor, especially not poor people, and no one should claim the title of "poor" because they need a fast doorway out of a conversation about harmful cycles they find themselves caught up in. People lean into their lack of money as a way to explain their participation in these unethical systems, "because that's all they can afford." But here's the thing: if you are buying clothing online multiple times

> "Being broke is a state; poverty is systemic."

a month, generally you aren't poor. In order to get a broader perspective of your place within global wealth, let's zoom out...

Let's look at Credit Suisse's Global Wealth Report from October 2020. There is a world wealth map from 2019, which measures the mean wealth of households. Countries in the Global North (such as the North Americas, Europe, etc.) tend to have considerably more wealth than countries in the Global South. Guess which countries these may be? Guess!

"Countries with average wealth below USD $5,000 comprise the final group, which is heavily concentrated in central Africa and central Asia." You mean, in places where our clothing is made, those people are among some of the poorest in the world? You mean, entire continents that, although they are resource-rich, aren't wealthy places? It's almost as though this map of global wealth is actually one that represents a history of pillaging and colonization that had led to these countries being financially disempowered and left stuck in a system that feeds their economy just enough to keep them poor and not rich enough to take their power back.

The report goes on: "The contrast between those who have access to an emergency buffer and those who do not is evident at the best of times. When, as now in 2020, vast numbers of individuals are simultaneously subjected to an adverse shock, the importance of household wealth is difficult to overestimate. Countries with low wealth face greater exposure to the negative consequences of COVID-19. Individuals with low wealth have many fewer options when facing emergency situations."

According to Marieke Eyskoot in *This Is a Good Guide for a*

Sustainable Lifestyle, if you look at what garment workers make, the current minimum wage per month is:

US$82 (68 Euros/£59) in Sri Lanka
US$103 (85 Euros/£74) in Bangladesh
US$132 (109 Euros/£95) in India
US$200 (165 Euros/£144) in Cambodia
US$201 (166 Euros/£145) in Indonesia

And you thought you had it bad and you were broke? Even taking into account the comparative cost of living, these wages are low. So, please let's stop with the "they should be grateful for a job" talk. These aren't good jobs. This is the stuff that perpetuates poverty and makes it an endless well that's impossible to climb out of, because it keeps you in it. None of your family can climb out of it. And you can never save enough to get yourself out of it either. It keeps you living in poverty, and it keeps generations and countries poor.

Meanwhile, in the nations where the majority of the products made in these poor countries get exported to, "sixty-two percent of the world's millionaires continue to reside in Europe or North America, with almost 40 percent of these millionaires calling the United States home," according to Inequality.org.

According to Oxfam in their list of "5 Shocking Facts About Extreme Global Inequality," "Almost half of humanity is living on less than $5.50 a day." (Not to be down on my generation, but that's what some of us spend on a latte, *and* I'm not mad at you for that either. You deserve that latte; that's not the reason you can't buy a house.) But this is subsistence rather than a living wage. And the truth is, this polarization of wealth isn't just found in different countries; it is also found within the same country and, indeed, city.

Inequality.org adds: "The United States has more wealth than any other nation. But America's top-heavy distribution of wealth leaves typical American adults with far less wealth than their counterparts in other industrial nations." (That's why you don't have a house.)

The wealth distribution is wide, and only increases to get wider, meaning the people with the most money get more money and the people with no money get even less. The gap isn't being bridged through these systems of capitalization and commerce; these are, in fact, only enforcing the gap. Those at the top profit from those at the bottom's lack of wealth. And those at the bottom are reliant on those at the top. It is a sort of feudal system whereby the colonizers have taken people's lands and rented them back to them for the service of their work on their own lands.

Do you think a person who lives on $5.50 a day is buying multiple pieces of fast fashion a month? Because I certainly don't. If a person lives on $5.50 a day, let's put their annual salary at $2,000 a year, which, of course, is not guaranteed as they are unlikely to have job security.

But did you know that according to Pew Research Center in their analysis from 2015, 56 percent of Americans were in the world's high-income group in 2011? It is even more illuminating to hear that "On a global scale, the vast majority of Americans are either in the upper-middle income or high-income group. And many Americans who are classified as 'poor' by the US government would be classed as middle income globally."

Now, of course, income inequality is still a battleground that

Americans are constantly fighting, but in the eyes of the rest of the world...we're at the top of the chain. And it's not just America, it's Europe, too. From the aforementioned report, "The majority of Americans are part of the global high-income population that resides almost exclusively in Europe and North America. These two regions accounted for 87 percent of the global high-income population in 2011." The inequality is pretty clear.

What's even more frightening is how many Americans have little control over their spending. According to Healthline.com, "Shopping addiction, also known as compulsive buying disorder, or compulsive shopping, affects about 18 million adults in the United States. It's described as the compulsion to spend money, regardless of need or financial means." Essentially, they are addicted to a cycle of buying that never filters down the chain and only ever filters up.

All of this overconsumption means that we may well feel "poor" and less well-off than others, because we simply have too much stuff and not enough assets that accrue over time rather than lose their RRP (recommended retail price) as soon as you take the label off of them. We have bought too much. The truth is that we have extreme economic privilege on a comparative global scale (even though, yes, there are times when we all naturally feel a bit skint). And some of us truly *are* skint (living around or below the poverty line). The problem is, you probably feel skint (or are actually "poor") because the money isn't fairly divided, even in economically privileged countries. The divides that exist at the bottom also exist in the middle and at the top. Think of them like wealth safeguards that no one can get past, because the system has been built to enforce and protect them.

WHO'S CONSUMING THE MOST?

According to a piece written by the business network Common Objective in 2018, US consumers appeared to be the keenest shoppers: on average a US consumer purchased one mid-priced item of clothing per week: the calls are coming from inside the house. Although China had the largest number of purchases, due to its large population, an average individual consumer in China spent just under a quarter of the amount that the average US consumer spent—and bought twenty-three fewer items per year.

This means the indications are that the US still reigns in fast fashion consumption; although over in Europe, a House of Commons committee in 2018 revealed the UK "consumes clothes" faster than any other country in Europe. The calls are only getting louder. "The UK's contribution is enormous," Lucy Siegle confirmed this in the *Guardian* in a report in June 2019. "Not only did we invent fast fashion, but our fashion consumers are among the most voracious in the world. One in three young women, the biggest segment of consumers, consider garments worn once or twice to be old. UK consumers sent 300,000 tons of textiles to be burned or dumped in landfill in 2018."

Our disposable treatment of clothing is a recent development and has fed into why this has become a crisis of such huge proportions. We can't seem to stop spending, and we can't seem to stop wanting to buy at cheaper and cheaper prices (which knocks on to the bottom line of those at the bottom). We consume and we consume and we consume, while not giving much thought to the lifespan of our clothes, or other people on our planet, or our planet itself.

For all those who care about the climate emergency, Donald Trump was the worst thing that could have happened to the planet. If you take all of the other horrible things out of the Trump administration—the racism, the bigotry, the harm done to immigrants, the sexism, the golf trips, the bad foreign policies—it's arguable that the worst was the damage done to the fight against climate emergency. In January 2021 the *New York Times* reported that the man "rolled back more than 100 environmental rules." If we know we're kind of down to the wire with climate emergency, it's fair to say that white voters (who voted overwhelmingly for Trump) would rather risk us all going up in flames than not lean into white supremacy.

Our climate emergency is everyone's problem, and many of us from the wealthier nations have, sadly, impacted others who haven't contributed in the same way to what will happen to our planet. And, even more tragically, it will probably happen to them sooner. Higher temperatures and more erratic weather systems will mostly appear in their continents first. In order to change that outcome, we first have to change these very systems.

WHAT GLOBAL WEALTH IS DOING TO THE PLANET

Which news do you want first? The bad news or the *really* bad news?

Let's start with the really bad news. Quick, like ripping a Band-Aid off. All these systems we're about to discuss are killing us. We are in trouble. And when I say we, I mean all humans. Actually, all life on Earth. **This Is Not A Drill.** Some people on the planet have all the natural resources, and these mostly exist in the Global South, but the other half of the planet lives off them as they don't have enough of these resources to keep the planet going, which ensures that none of us will be here in the future. And it's because of all these systems of oppression, which we can't seem to move away from, mixed in with a heavy mixture of capitalism and consumerism, that (per the World Wildlife Fund):

- The Arctic is melting.
- The Great Barrier Reef is bleaching.
- The Amazon rain forest is being bulldozed.
- Entire seas (like the Aral Sea) are disappearing.
- The world's oceans have lost 50 percent of their oxygen in just fifty years.
- We've lost half our wildlife in the past forty years.
- Approximately 7 million deaths occur annually, 4 million of which are connected to air pollution.
- Pollution has affected so much that distance and clarity of what we see is reduced by 70 percent across the world.

Once we fall out of harmony with our surroundings, equilibrium is unbalanced and the ecosystem which created and sustained life is disconnected. At the time of writing, we have less than ten years to get our act together. Some believe the 2030 deadline will be too late. We're past the point of not seeing the temperature climb degree by degree in many parts of the world; and many places, particularly areas where marginalized people live, are already seeing the effects of climate emergency. It's not in the future, it's here now. We can do our best to mitigate it, but that looks like action from everyone, both citizens and lawmakers.

A Note on Band-Aids and Theft

I was in my teens when I realized that Band-Aids (adhesive bandages, or plasters in the UK) were supposed to look like skin... white skin, not my skin, and that's living in a white supremacy for you. Because Black people don't get hurt and require bandages or anything. Just kidding, we do. We just didn't get the luxury of being included in the adhesive bandage conversation until recent years. Not too long ago, a prominent supermarket chain launched bandages that came in a range of skin tones—including darker skin—which ostensibly had never been done before. The supermarket chain reached out to a well-known content creator of color, offering her a single box of these bandages in exchange for her promotion on Instagram... something surely worth a few thousand dollars, but they only wanted to give her a £3 (approximately $4.20) box. This person creates content full-time, but you want to give her a product worth £3? *Oh, okay.* Writer Clark-

And guess what's aiding and abetting the deterioration? Extracting resources. As a matter of fact, according to a report by the United Nations Environment Programme in March 2019, extracting and processing resources is causing 90 percent of biodiversity loss and water stress on our planet. So that's everything we buy and consume. With a special nod to the fashion industry. The clothes you wear. That cheeky little purchase of a dress you might not even wear is playing its role.

Indeed, Dana Thomas cited in her book *Fashionopolis* that 10 isha Kent has been vocal about how in this case, a Black creative actually came up with the idea of inclusive bandages first, and the supermarket ripped off the idea and claimed it as their own. All while asking Black content creators to support their efforts... for free.

They could have licensed these bandages from the Black-owned brand. They could have paid people to promote both the product and their good efforts to champion businesses owned by marginalized people. But no, no, let's just go at it on our own, cutting corners every step of the way, while stepping on people and devaluing labor. But this isn't anything out of the norm. This happens literally *all the time* to Black people, particularly in the fashion industry. We are both underrepresented and constantly left out of the conversation, all while having our ideas and identities pilfered for... consumption. But that has always been the way, when our society is built on a system of racism in which only certain voices are elevated and praised.

percent of global carbon emissions are from the textile industry. What's more, as Lauren Bravo mentions in her book *How to Break Up with Fast Fashion*, "At its current rate, the fashion industry is projected to use 35 percent more land to grow fibers by 2030. That's an extra 115 million hectares of land that could otherwise be used to grow food, or left to protect biodiversity."

In *Fashionopolis*, Thomas also states that the clothing industry is responsible for 20 percent of industrial water pollution. And unlike food, you can't eat your clothes in an emergency, which doesn't help anyone, as the future we're looking at currently involves both food and water scarcity on a planet where clean water should be a human right for everyone (and already isn't). And what's more is that the fashion industry is projected to keep moving further along on this path if we don't start to change things.

It's in the waters.

Dear Reader,

It's my displeasure to introduce you to "The World's Most Polluted River," otherwise known as the Citarum River in Indonesia (my information is coming from an amazing Deutsche Welle [DW] documentary available to view on YouTube). Let me tell you a little bit about the Citarum River so you two can get better acquainted. The river is a source of electricity and water for thousands, if not millions, of people. Water for agriculture. Water to bathe in. Water to wash your dishes in. Water to drink.

At the source of the river the water is beautiful and clear, but as it flows, you begin to notice things take a darker turn. Waste disposal in Indonesia is still somewhat underdeveloped, which means in some places the river is filled to the brim with trash. It's a pretty grim look in comparison to the pristine water upstream.

But it gets far worse. As you begin to approach the factories, the quality of water changes, but in particular you notice the change in its color. It's now filled with chemicals. And the effects hit children the hardest. According to an article by the World Health Organization titled "Lead Poisoning and Health" from August 2019, "Young children are particularly vulnerable to the toxic effects of lead and can suffer profound and permanent adverse health effects, particularly affecting the development of the brain and nervous system." Most people living alongside the river use it as their primary water source.

It's very hard to access detailed information on the effects that this contamination has had on the people that rely on the river as a life source...but where there's smoke, there's fire. In the DW documentary, activist Deni Riswandani, along with other citizens, has tried to join the dots between the water source and the source of local health problems. "In this region there are 500 textile manufacturers located along the Citarum. And they pour their sewage directly into the river. On average each of these plants dispose of 1,300 liters (approximately 343 gallons) of wastewater, a day." So that's 650,000 liters (approximately 171,711 gallons) of wastewater flowing into the Citarum daily. "Seventy-five percent of [the factories'] production is destined for export, mainly to the American and European markets."

The water has since been tested by a lab, and the results are dire. No wonder the children in certain villages are sick. Kang Yusef, a local farmer, demonstrates how his rice crops (which are surrounded by factories) are rotting at the roots, because the water that irrigates his rice is purple. Guess what shows up in rice that is tested? Chromium. Lead.

In the documentary, Professor Sunardi Sudianto of the Institute of Ecology, Padjadjaran University, says, "If the government puts very strict standards, then investors will not come to Indonesia. But you know if there is no standard, then we sacrifice the people."

Why is this a choice that countries are having to make, and why are "investors" in such a strong-arm position of power, when they need this labor? Well, that's because global demand is so high that the textile production in Indonesia is expected to increase by 75 percent by 2030.

Since the making of the documentary, the Indonesian government has planned for a historic cleanup of the Citarum River, and the president has promised that the water will be drinkable by 2025. I'm left feeling angry. Where are the big brands and businesses who profit enormously from this environmental disaster? Because whose fault is it really? The people of Indonesia, or the companies that profit while the communities that line the river essentially perish?

The truth is someone along this river is getting very, very rich. And it's not the person being forced to drink, farm, and bathe in wastewater. And it's not the Indonesian factory workers or owners. Why aren't these billion-dollar companies being asked to clean up their mess? Why won't these companies simply manufacture in their home countries?

The stench of factory textile waste pouring into a local river would usually cause citizens to riot in the street. No one actually wants wastewater flowing into their water supply at any cost... However, the Citarum is someone else's local river. Note that in February of 2021 Thames Water in the UK was fined £2.3 million ($3.2 million) for water pollution (and a whopping £20 million [$28 million] in 2017 for pumping out untreated sewage). We shouldn't be okay with this happening anywhere.

In a court of law, a corporation will only act in its own best interest. Which means that contrary to popular belief (what billionaires would lead you to believe), no one manufactures overseas to be altruistic and bring jobs to the people. There's always something in it for them, and it's not exactly a win–win situation.

Indonesia is just one manufacturing hub in this picture. What about Bangladesh? India? El Salvador? Cambodia? Vietnam? Rest assured, there are similar stories in all of these nations if you just look hard enough.

Dear reader, would you drink from the Citarum River? Closer to home, would you drink the water in Flint, Michigan? Or take your refillable water bottle down to the Thames?

WHAT DO WE CHANGE?

1. The way we buy.
2. The amount we purchase.
3. How those within the supply chain are treated.
4. Ourselves and how we participate in and perpetuate this system.

The irony of it all is that, when the Amazon burns or a brush-fire happens in Australia, and some cheesy company that constantly pushes clothing through social media decides to make a *t-shirt* and donate a portion of the proceeds to fighting the environmental disaster, that really is the very, very least they could be doing. In fact, there is a lot more they *could* be doing. (And heads up, none of it looks like making yet another pointless t-shirt for consumption.)

They could make a start with making things more sustainable by making them durable. If the clothing they produced were of higher quality, then the average person wouldn't have to buy 60 percent more items of clothing every year, which they will keep for about half as long as people did fifteen years ago, which in turn produces immense volumes of textile waste, as the research Timeout for Fast Fashion by Greenpeace suggested in 2016. Of course, they'll claim they're doing that, but…you regularly push consumers to consume through social media, so what's your goal here again?

NON-REGULATION AND THE HUMAN COST

When people say the system is broken, it's a tad bit misleading. The system of extraction and exploitation was built by centuries of exploitation and colonialism. The "system" is actually working just as it's supposed to, with little legality and liability, few safety nets, zero responsibility for those making billions of dollars at the top. The system isn't broken at all. This is exactly how it was built to work—exploitation and destruction of the world's most marginalized people for the benefit of others. Because the fashion industry never improves; it just moves to another country, where it's easier to exploit people with even fewer safety nets for those doing the hardest labor.

Regulation for some is not regulation for all. What is regulation, you ask? It's the idea that, say, you're working in a factory around dangerous machinery and you get injured or killed… there's responsibility for you from your employer. When we move manufacturing to avoid regulation in order to secure lower costs, we're opening up a world of harm to those who are making the goods.

> "Regulation for some is not regulation for all."

Back in civics class, we were taught all about the Triangle Shirtwaist Factory fire, which was the deadliest industrial disaster in New York City. It took place in 1911 and killed 146 workers (mostly immigrant Jewish and Italian women) and, after much mobilization, led to a spate of new regulations being created to protect industry workers in the US, in particular, safe working practices and the well-being of those under employment. It is all well and good that we are taught that this built a society where Americans can flourish in safety, but what was left unspoken is that today you can't get the vast majority of the products in your house manufactured in America, because all that manufacturing moved overseas.

Manufacturing moved to China, India, Bangladesh, Cambodia, Sri Lanka, the Philippines, and Pakistan. You know, all the places where all the people of color live. And whenever workers in those industries rise up and demand more, it moves again. And to date, the accidents and fires that have raged unregulated are continuing—out of our sight but still happening nonetheless. Currently the manufacturing industry has its eyes on various countries in Africa, with Ethiopia being seen as the next hub. But, at the time of this writing in 2021, a fire recently broke out in a factory in Egypt, killing at least twenty.

So, we have exported the mess out, but it is still happening on the planet we share. In her groundbreaking book *To Die For*, Lucy Siegle explains just how dramatically the fast fashion system has sped up. Previously a garment factory would have been asked by a retailer to manufacture 40,000 garments over a matter of months, but today it's a much shorter time frame and a lower commitment, as "thirty thousand will be ordered last minute," often directly ripped off what a celebrity has been seen wearing. We witnessed this in BBC's *Breaking Fashion*, a TV show about the ultra-fast fashion brand In The Style, in which one episode documents an extremely quick turnover of a bodysuit inspired by one worn by Kylie Jenner. The turnover of goods is ultra-fast in order to capture the zeitgeist of the moment, with the aim of getting the sale before people move on to the next thing.

Everything is happening more quickly, everyone needs more of it, and it all needs to be at the cheapest price point for the consumer. Of course, something has to give. We can't accelerate to satisfy our needs this quickly without someone bearing the brunt. This hyper-inflation of want reflects how our consumer habits have changed. We want immediate gratification because of our endemic short-termism, which leaves us on a collision course with the rest of humanity and the planet. There is no equilibrium in this hyper-acceleration.

Every year, human lives are lost due to the fashion industry and the general negligence that happens behind the scenes. And sadly, those lives are always marginalized BIPOC. In 2013, when the eight-story Dhaka garment factory called Rana Plaza collapsed in Bangladesh, it killed 1,134 people and injured more than 2,500 others. The fact that cracks had been spotted days before, and the ground-floor plaza and bank had been closed, did not prevent the factory owners from asking their garment workers to come into work. When the building collapsed, there were multiple reasons why it happened: the building had been converted from commercial to industrial use, it had been built over a pond, and it had had several new floors added without structural planning or approval. Why had all these things been allowed? Because of a lack of regulation. And it is in factories like these that the vast majority of the clothes that you and I buy are being made.

This isn't new either. People working in unsafe, dangerous, and brutal conditions have always been there, helping you—and some of your ancestors—live the lives you and they have done.

That's who picked your cotton.

That's who farmed your cotton.

That's who was inhaling fumes for sandblasted denim.

That's whose river for drinking water is polluted.

That's who works in today's sweatshops.

That's who inspires so many a streetwear trend (Fashion Nova, what's good?).

And that story is a tale as old as time.

When you begin to look into the story of the textile industry, you find yourself looking at the story of exploitation and colonialism. It is expansive, and it affects many different identities in very different, unique, and incredibly harmful ways. So much of our past is written in our present, and all I ask is that it doesn't get to take a hold and control our future, too. We need new rules in order to safeguard those who deserve a better future.

And one future I am keen to avoid is the one where humanity didn't manage to turn this ship around, we're all gone, and our planet is left depleted and stressed. Imagine that visitors from another galaxy visit Earth to see what happened, and they find oceans full of plastic bags and mountains of rotting polyester fiber (aka single-use dresses). The conclusion they might draw from all of that is that we actually shopped ourselves to death.

See? You're mortified, too.

CLIMATE EMERGENCY AND MARGINALIZED PEOPLE

When I was a teenager in 1995, Hurricane Marilyn blew through St. Thomas in the Virgin Islands and decimated everything in its path. While hurricanes are a part of island life, they're only expected to get worse as we descend further into the climate emergency. Much of my family on my dad's side lives in St. Thomas (it was also where my parents met, and it was a hurricane that forced my mother to say, "Let's go"). My grammy's home was decimated. Family photos and heirlooms were destroyed. She was stateside at the time, caring for my ailing uncle, and she never returned to her home. Her home had gone.

At the time of this writing, much of Puerto Rico is still without power from Hurricane Maria.

In 2020 EcoWatch reported that flooding in China caused $32 billion in damages, while the *Hindustan Times* noted that extreme weather events in India have affected 75 percent of the country's districts. We're talking droughts, floods, cyclones. Countries such as South Sudan, Kenya, and Somalia are seeing unprecedented rainfall and even more flooding. Rising sea levels will affect Indigenous people everywhere and have already affected those in eastern Canada. The Climate Justice Resilience Fund stated in Climate Home News in 2019 that, "For Indigenous peoples in eastern Canada, rising sea levels have led to the salination of freshwater, which in turn affects food security and traditional medicines. In the north, temperature rise has seen disappearing ice roads not only threaten transport systems, but also create profoundly negative impacts on the mental health of increasingly isolated communities."

It is clear that those who are already bracing for the impact of climate change, and trying to mitigate against it, have actually contributed the least to patterns that are driving the emergency. In 2019, Yessenia Funes, on the science and technology blog Gizmodo, wrote that, "Though countries on the African continent have contributed very little to global warming, they are among the most vulnerable to the changes happening. What's happening in East Africa right now shows what that vulnerability looks like. Countries there have been dealing with extreme rainfall for months."

Mary Anne Hitt, director of the Sierra Club's Beyond Coal Campaign, notes in her piece "Beyond Coal" in *All We Can Save*: "The world's climate scientists are clear that it's essential for the developed nations of the world to phase out coal by 2030 to keep global temperatures below critical thresholds. So far, we are on track to do that here in the United States. If we get our own house in order, innovate affordable solutions, and demonstrate that people can enjoy a high quality of life in a decarbonized economy, that will accomplish far more than endless hand-wringing about China and India. Leadership is best shown through action."

While India and China might have their environmental damage to contend with, let's not forget these countries both export a lot of goods *today* that are consumed by you and me. Perhaps their footprint would be lower without this industry set up to feed our needs. So often, the conversation surrounding climate emergency looks pretty white, and the lens through which we see these disasters is always centered on problems close to home; like, per the United States Environmental Protection Agency (EPA), "Since the late 1970s, the United States has warmed faster than the global rate," or "there has never been a hotter summer," but what about the heatwaves that are scorching the land in Africa, what about the deserts this heat is enlarging, and the huge cost to life this comes with? Why don't we see much of this on our news or in our headlines? It's because this side of climate change doesn't serve us. When the Ugandan climate activist Vanessa Nakate holds cardboard placards up on her Instagram page reading "It's getting hot in here," are we truly listening, or are we wondering about more fertile crops that we might grow in ten years?

Indeed, as climate scientist Katharine Hayhoe has written in "How to Talk About Climate Change" in *All We Can Save*, "The eighty-five lowest emitting countries in the world, the Climate Vulnerable Forum estimates, who have contributed virtually nothing to the problem, will bear 40 percent of the economic losses and 80 percent of the resulting deaths from human-induced climate change. That is absolutely not fair."

Marginalized people have been conscientious stewards of the environment, whether we're looking at North American Indigenous people (they weren't the ones who almost killed off all the buffalo and, when it comes to protecting our water from pipelines, you couldn't look to better role models). When we look to the Amazon, we see Indigenous people there fighting on the front lines to protect their homes, which are the lungs of our planet. We all benefit from their labor. And when we look at America, Black people have also been incredible stewards of the land (whether we wanted to be or not). We know how to grow things; I mean, it's said we smuggled watermelon seeds to the Americas, and they thrived there. And sadly enough, we're often not in a position to do more because of disenfranchisement.

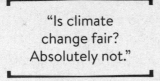

"Is climate change fair? Absolutely not."

Is climate change fair?

Absolutely not.

The poorest and most vulnerable among us, those who have done the least to contribute to the problem, are the most affected. These include the women and children that the shelter organization Adsum supports in Halifax, Nova Scotia; farmers struggling to raise their crops in East Africa; Bangladeshis losing their land to sea-level rise and erosion; and Arctic peoples whose traditions are threatened and whose homes are being displaced by rising seas and thawing permafrost. The carbon footprint of these groups is minuscule. As Katharine Hayhoe noted on the website Chatelaine in April 2019, "They've contributed so little to the problem, yet they bear the brunt of the impacts."

Climate change is hurting marginalized people, and yet we're consistently left out of the Global North's conversation. But how does it affect us more? To answer this, I reached out to my friend, and the co-editor of the amazing and groundbreaking book *All We Can Save: Truth, Courage, and Solutions for the Climate Crisis*, Dr. Ayana Elizabeth Johnson—a marine biologist and co-host of the podcast *To Save a Planet*.

In the introduction to her book, Dr. Johnson breaks it down: "Climate change is a powerful 'threat multiplier,' making existing vulnerabilities and injustices worse. Especially under conditions of poverty, women and girls face greater risk of displacement or death from extreme weather disasters. Early marriage and sex work—sometimes last-resort survival strategies—have been tied to droughts and floods."

It's good to look at and unpack the term "threat multiplier." People who are already marginalized aren't going to have the resources to help support them through this, nor do they have the support from their governments or economies. Because of intersecting oppression anyone who is marginalized will have that status exasperated under a climate emergency. Added to

A Note on Names and Representation

Now, the night before I got to chat with Dr. Johnson, I was talking with my mother, and our conversation went...well, it went like:

"I'm interviewing someone I admire tomorrow for the book—a climate scientist! Guess what her name is."

"What is it?"

"Ayana!!!"

"Girl, GET OUT!"

You see, my sisters' names are Ayana and Aisha. Our names are forever mispronounced and considered too Black for a society colonized by whiteness. We grew up searching for our names in license-plate kiosks and shops at amusement parks, so much so that on one birthday I asked that my parents take me to the mall, and there I had one mini license plate *made* in a mall kiosk (I'm sure it's still floating around my parents' house somewhere). Colonialism is taking identities and forcing them to fit that of the dominant caste, and it can be something like a name. Like Kunta

which, due to the legendary work of Dr. Robert Bullard, we now know facts such as that in the US the authorities often deliberately chose Black neighborhoods as toxic waste sites and places where city dumps were built. Why? Because they could. Because the system allowed them to do this.

Mary Anne Hitt recalls in *All We Can Save*: "I'll never forget my trips to River Rouge, Michigan, on the outskirts of Detroit,

Kinte in *Roots*, or forcing Indigenous kids into boarding schools and stripping them of all their identity and culture, including their names. These are acts of violence, and it shows up in our modern culture by folks with non-Western names being othered or living a life of constant mispronunciation.

I once corrected a gymnastics coach on my name in class. Instead of thanking me, she disciplined me in the middle of the class and said she wouldn't be using anyone's name for the rest of class, and they could all thank me for it. This caused one white classmate to join in on the bullying and chiding demonstrated by our coach. I sat out the rest of the class and cried. I shortly quit gymnastics, even though I loved gymnastics. I was eight.

But this launched the moment when I kind of stopped correcting the world on my name. At my wedding, a couple of my friends noted that they had been saying my name differently from the way my parents say it (hard J vs. soft J; it's a softer J)... I assured them it was okay because I didn't correct them—mostly because I was afraid to. Names matter. As does representation.

where two aging coal plants next to neighborhoods and playgrounds were operating without modern air pollution controls known as 'scrubbers' and making people sick in this predominantly African American community. My heart was broken by stories of mothers who lost their children to asthma attacks, school kids leaving soccer fields in ambulances, and regulators who had failed these families for decades."

In 2020, a coroner found that the death of nine-year-old Ella Kissi-Debrah in London was caused by air pollution and severe asthma. Kissi-Debrah was Black. She also only lived a few miles from me. I had asthma as a child but didn't struggle with it much in adulthood. I moved back to London in late 2017, and my hacking cough returned. Today I keep an inhaler in my house just in case. There is not a doubt in my mind that moving back to London, particularly the neighborhood I live in, has made my asthma more of a presence in my life again. What are we doing to these children? Why are we allowing those in more marginalized spaces to be exposed to more danger? I am sorry, it is the same answer. It has happened because it could happen. Because the system allowed this to happen.

Over in the United States, in Crossett, Arkansas, the Koch brothers were two rich men who built a variety of businesses, and also built a political network that loved to funnel money into advertising that served conservative causes and helped their own businesses to escape accountability. I like to think that one of my goals in my lifetime is to lead a life so good that few would have cause to celebrate my death. But when one of the brothers passed away... many people did not lament the passing. You see, the Koch brothers were no strangers to dumping toxic waste in both Black and Latino neighborhoods (the *Guardian* reported, "People who live in Crossett [Arkansas] blame the mill for the heedless dumping of cancer-causing chemicals they say pollutes drinking water and shortens already straitened lives"). Local Nick Limbeck was quoted in *In These Times* magazine saying, "The black community knows who their enemy is—now the Latino community is seeing who their enemy is, as [Chicago mayor Rahm Emanuel] is helping the Koch brothers dump toxic waste in Latino neighborhoods." All while the brothers donated millions to hospitals and museums, which they put their names on, and gave money to my favorite ballet companies. Those sorts of moves only serve to obscure the harm done elsewhere. It's similar to those multinational clothing companies donating to the World Health Organization while forcing their employees to work during a global pandemic when we should all be sheltering at home (if we can). And, of course, the same brothers funded climate-denial media, too.

In 2016, Sean McElwee wrote on the Al Jazeera America website that "Lee Fang, a journalist at The Intercept, has written about how major donors like the Koch brothers have funneled millions into organizations that deny climate change and actively work to oppose climate legislation. He recently uncovered a massive network of secret political spending aimed at funding climate change denial."

THE TOLL

Whether it is a pipeline running through Indigenous neighborhoods. It's Indigenous people. From the Dakota and Keystone pipelines to Enbridge's Line 3 pipeline, the war for the Indigenous to protect the land which is rightfully theirs from fossil fuel companies wages on.

Whether it is a coal industry that harms many people, including white people. Those people whose survival currently depends on their remaining working for this industry, and those who actively fight against the coal industry because they know the long-term health effects it has on all who surround the mining areas.

Whether it is neighborhood zoning. Black people who know that they are more likely to end up living with a dump nearby and with fewer trees.

Whether it is water insecurity. Cotton farmers who are already struggling.

FEMINISM AND CLIMATE CHANGE

Climate change is a feminist issue. Let's unpack that. Women and marginalized genders all over the world will be impacted the hardest. Dr. Ayana Elizabeth Johnson explains that it can be something simple, such as gender roles:

> Like women who are responsible for collecting water for their families or wood for cooking, and how much harder that is because of the way our climate has changed. But there's a lot of other layers to it. It connects to domestic abuse, for example… And the insecurities that arise in communities around food scarcity or water scarcity, and that bubbles up the tensions in all these negative ways.
>
> More than ever, it's important for women to be involved in the solutions. I learned a lot about how legislation where women are involved…well, let's just say, we get things done. There's social science data around this. There are statistics, and this has been rigorously studied: if you have more women in parliaments, you pass more environmental protections, stronger environmental protections, [and] those get enforced more strongly. More nature areas are protected when you have women in positions of political and policy-making power. We

have just better outcomes for the health of life on Earth. So why would we not embrace that?

I see this in so many of the amazing writers, speakers and educators who I'm lucky to share space with on social media. In the conversation battling the ills of fast fashion, it's always a group of us speaking up, and those loud voices tend to be a lot of women. It makes me feel proud. But we should definitely be in the front row surrounding law-making as well, as it affects us too. And sadly there still isn't the most even balance of power there, if you look at the various governments of the world...We think about the Paris Agreements and the UN Climate Negotiations, the successful round of that was led by women; and in this upcoming one, only 15 percent of the negotiators at this moment are women, which seems to me like another recipe for disaster.

Yeah, we definitely need to address that.
Dr. Johnson continues:

But if we want to be a part of envisioning a new way of living on the planet, thinking about the social, political, economic transformation, cultural transformation that we need, we need women to have an equal seat at the table leading that. You could argue more than equal seats, given that what history has shown us is not working. Why not try something new?

We already see who is leading the fight for garment workers' rights all over the world, and guess what...it's women! Dr. Johnson says,

Until we looked into that research, I thought it was just the right thing to do. Gender equality, racial equality, it's just the right thing to do. But as we've learned with racial diversity, having that leads to better outcomes. It leads to better decisions within corporations and all sorts of institutions. It is a quantifiable benefit to have diversity along the lines of race, and the same, it turns out, is true of gender. It's just a freebie! We should take it!

I hear you asking, what are the solutions? Ayana believes that it involves the harnessing of everyone's superpowers. Listen, folks, if a gal who lived in her parents' basement repeatedly in adulthood can grow a platform and inform the public about the ills of an industry she once loved and write a book...well, trust me, I believe you definitely have a superpower, too. And most of it starts with finding your voice.

There is absolutely room for all of us in this conversation. And we should all be contributing. If you live on planet Earth and breathe oxygen, you're an environmentalist, whether you like it or not, because you are breathing the same stuff as every single other person on this planet (and, if you are lucky, you are breathing in some of the cleaner variety).

> "There is absolutely room for all of us in this conversation. And we should all be contributing."

I like to think of my grandfather William Barber II, who organized buses from York, Pennsylvania, to march on Washington, and worked for the United States Environmental Protection Agency (dude was way ahead of his time without even knowing it). I don't think he set out to be an "activist," but he just knew that he didn't like the current state of the world, and he was going to do something about that. Being a Black person in the air force only to return home and be told to get to the back of the bus might have had something to do with that. When injustice is prevalent everywhere you look, your back is definitely against the wall. With climate emergency coming for all of us, I would argue that all of our backs are against the wall. Time to swing back.

So, I guess the next question is…what can we save, exactly?

Per Dr. Johnson, "We're probably going to avoid complete fire and brimstone and *Day After Tomorrow* apocalypse, but we're definitely not going to have pristine perfect nature with eight billion people on the planet. But what is in between…that we could have, that is still very much up for grabs. And the difference between one and a half degrees Celsius of planetary warming and four degrees is an astronomical difference in terms of quality of life, and so the more that we can figure out how to harness the ingenuity, creativity, skills, expertise that exist in abundance within humanity and help everyone figure out where they fit in, then that's the solution."

What needs to happen then is this.

We all need to:

- Recognize what we can do.
- See and observe our intersections.
- Recognize what we're good at and apply it where necessary.

So come on in.

Wade in the water with us.

If we all use our hands and minds, we can keep the water just fine.

(NB: At the time of writing this I was listening to the recording of my interview with Dr. Johnson, and she left off by telling folks, "Come on in, the water's fine." As I was transcribing her words and smiling, "Wade in the Water" by the Ramsey Lewis Trio came on the radio randomly. If there were ever an epic song to write about Black people I admire, my amazing grandparents, and the important work they did in their lives, this was the song! The idea of listening to a song my grandfather no doubt enjoyed, while typing about his important contributions and writing about the climate emergency, I don't know…just feels powerful.)

RACISM AND WEALTH

It's an entitlement to believe, despite all evidence to the contrary, that we can go on living as we have been. When I first raised my voice, I felt as though white people were patting me on the head and saying, "That's nice, little Black girl." But the truth is, more often than not, it's BIPOC people who end up disenfranchised. It's BIPOC who end up with the waste sites in their backyard. It's BIPOC making the clothes, and it's BIPOC in the Global South who mitigate the world's waste. And it's *not* fair.

Whether or not you're ready to admit it, see it, or open your eyes to it, racism is all around us. It is in the everyday interactions we all have, and it is embedded in the structures of our society. It is also besties with colonialism: racism and colonialism support and lift up one another.

We need to critically examine the law as it intersects with issues of race and to challenge mainstream approaches to racial justice. And that involves tearing at the foundation that some of the most powerful countries are built upon... exposing the false narratives that dismiss the existence of white supremacy and the effects it has on our modern-day world. And certain people (white people) don't like that very much, because that looks like a call for a radical shift in power.

> "We need to critically examine the law as it intersects with issues of race and to challenge mainstream approaches to racial justice."

And, for the people at the back, white privilege doesn't mean that you haven't faced adversity: it means that you've not faced certain *structural* inequalities because of the color of your skin, and having that inherent privilege means that, more often than not, you can't see it until it's pointed out to you. So maybe that's why these conversations about race might feel so new to you (and so validating to the vast majority of non-white people), because you didn't have to face them on a daily basis, they weren't part of your childhood, they weren't your lived experience.

Race and racism *is* all around us, because it is a part of the founding system in which we all live. Race has been used to oppress and exploit people of color from the conception of our laws and legal institutions. So they, too, are inherently racist because they create, protect, and uphold social, economic, and political inequalities, all because white people were on the team with the advantage. The truth is, elementary school education of the past did us a *massive* disservice by speaking about race as if we shouldn't see it, as if it should be "invisible." The whole notion of "I don't see race" became used to dismiss *huge* structural inequalities that exist within the very framework of the globalized world. Just because you might not see it doesn't mean that it isn't there. Often the most insidious parts of our society are those that are inherent within the very fabric of it, and, in fact, the more advantage people seem to have the more they are blinded to the gaping chasms that exist under their noses.

And while anyone can experience poverty, regardless of the color of their skin, when it comes to who has wealth and who doesn't, race plays a massive role in why certain countries (looking at you, colonial Europe) dominate global financial markets.

Candice Brathwaite, in her book *I Am Not Your Baby Mother*, said that "According to research from Legal and General and the economics consultancy Cebr in 2017, it was estimated that first-time buyers borrowed over six billion pounds from their parents that year alone. And yet according to a House of Commons report in June 2017, fewer than a third of black households are headed by owner-occupiers." Racism often determines how far you get in life, and whether or not you succeed at the things you want to do.

To use myself as an example when discussing this: I have wanted to be a writer (and work in the fashion industry) my whole life. However, I knew as a small Black child in the 1990s there was no place for my voice or my words. Everything about my station in life quietly signaled that to me. But the truth is, so many of the BIPOC writers I respect and admire have only had their success in the last ten years (particularly Black women). It seemed like there was a moment when I looked and suddenly the world was "letting us in." Imagine a world where these barriers weren't in place at all. Imagine a world where BIPOC parents didn't urge us to get degrees in fields where we could "actually get a job." These are the invisible barriers that rule our lives, which few people notice.

In 2021, I'm noticing that "Thirty Under Thirty" lists *are* looking more diverse than ever before. I'm seeing a lot of people who I know don't have much of a leg up finally being celebrated and getting their due! I'm finally seeing more people who look like me, and that fills me with joy. It seems like a move in the right direction, but I remember how those sorts of groupings made me feel when I was one of the "Millions Under Thirty Living with Their Parents." (I'm not knocking living with your parents, if you can do it...That's a privilege, but it still feels like failure when others around you are buying real estate.)

Until our society talks more openly about generational wealth and privilege, and who has it and who doesn't, these lists will come across as disingenuous. Some aren't talking about how they paid for their university, and how student loans impact what jobs they *have* to go for, and the length of time they can expose themselves to being jobless but chasing a dream risk. Few are talking about their family background (because often it then becomes illuminating how and why their station in life looks much different from your own). We can cheer for others, and I champion a society that does that. But I also champion a society where those we cheer for go, "I started this company with a loan from my parents, and not everyone has those opportunities and I get that." How many discuss whether they were educated in public schools or private schools, and the ways in which private education advanced them? We don't talk enough about power and resources, and who has access to a realm of possibility and who does not. I remember in the 1980s realizing that a few of my classmates didn't have computers at home. This lack already limited their knowledge of computer programs we learned about in our computer science class (anyone remember Logo?). Many were already behind, and I wasn't better at it than they were; I just had something they didn't, which put me ahead. These things matter pretty early in the game, but how often do we stop to even recognize that for a moment when praising the accomplishments of others?

I'm not saying you have to be ashamed of your wealth, but there's a slippery slope in between *omitting the truth* and *lying* about circumstances. The two are beginning to look the same. But you help no one when you do that. Certainly not your friend who doesn't have the same accomplishments and beats themselves up over it quietly. Being wealthy doesn't mean that your life hasn't had challenges. You can still be born into a crappy family surrounded by people who don't know how to love you the way you need to be loved. You're not exempt from depression. You can still have an unhappy childhood. But while all of those things can be true, one thing wealth gives you is access to resources aplenty—and things like healthcare and mental health services. And that's nothing to sniff at.

Let's put it in another way, if I can acknowledge that being able to travel at a young age changed my entire life trajectory (and it did), then certainly you can acknowledge that perhaps you didn't buy that entire house *all* by yourself.

I don't have white privilege, and not having it has greatly impacted my life and how I move through all these systems, but also how I'm viewed by the world. And this played into how I developed habits and insecurities that led me to escalated consumption. I didn't buy all those clothes because I needed them; I bought them because I wanted to be liked and treated decently in a world that constantly treats Black people like an afterthought while simultaneously putting us under a microscope. I'm considered a sustainability expert, and yet when I used to walk into clothes shops (pre-lockdown) to ask about sustainable clothing, white sales associates would talk to me like I just crawled out of a cave, like they really needed to educate "this Black woman," because there was no way I could possibly *know* what sustainability *even is*. I guess it's a modest step up from being followed around the store. Or maybe it's a new way of racial profiling.

As my friend Rachel Ricketts (no relation to Liz) says in her book *Do Better*, "The modern concept of race was created by and for the empowerment of those who qualify as white, and this is the heart of what racism is and how it operates. Contrary to dictionary definitions created by white people to maintain white innocence, racism is a global system of race-based hierarchy, oppression, and discrimination created by and for the benefit of white people (read that again)."

Because racism is everywhere, it applies to everything we examine (see page 125 on intersectionality). And if you think the conversation about race doesn't apply to the fashion industry, you'd be dead wrong. At a basic level, because most of the clothes are produced in the Global South by BIPOC, these clothes are consumed in the Global North by majority-white countries, and then when the clothes are unsold/used they are dumped right back on the Global South as "donations." When you see landfill sites of donations (the rubbish that covers the thirty acres at Dandora in Kenya, to name but one), you start to challenge the notion of "goodwill" donating. From start to finish this system exploits the people and land of BIPOCs. And why is this? Well, the answer is straightforwardly immoral: because the system *still* can get away with it.

But it isn't just the cycle of clothing that is systemically racist, it is also the fashion brands and the broader industry, including magazines, advertising, and social media campaigns. The *New York Times* did an illuminating profile in March 2021 on Black representation in the fashion industry, titled "The Fashion World Promised More Diversity. Here's What We Found," and the results were, as to be expected, disappointing: "Behind the scenes, there is little Black representation among the executives and designers leading these brands." And although in 2020 there was a push for more Black models, this only really came after the Black Square day (Blackout Tuesday) in June, and they wanted to capitalize on our movement. To this, I can only say:

WEAK WEAK WEAKSAUCE.

But back to my own set of privileges. As I mentioned, I don't have white privilege. But I have other privileges. I have socio-economic privilege (I'm not living paycheck to paycheck). I'm university-educated (definitely a privilege). I'm able-bodied. If you're sitting there and you're white and thinking, "How come I didn't see all of this before now?" don't feel like you're alone. Before I had friends with disabilities, I didn't exactly know to add audio descriptions to my photos on Instagram, or push for automatic video captions. But now I know. Because I listen to others at different intersections from my own. Think outside of your frame of reference, and think, *What don't I know?* and *What would that feel like?*

Know better.

Do better.

And constantly unpack yourself.

4

HOW THE FAST FASHION
SYSTEM WORKS

FIVE WORDS: Stop the war on want.

(But support the charity by the same name.)

The truth is that fast brands are so successful because they created this system of optimal buying. It's become normal to buy new stuff every week because they made it the norm. This "normal" is their business model. It's not our saving plan, that's for sure. Their creation of "consumer overload" is directly proportionate to our "consumer overdrafts." Overloading us with things we *need* to own next inflates their gross profit line and deflates our savings accounts. But we consumers are not the worst hit by this unsustainable supply chain, not by any stretch.

It shouldn't be like this. It never should have been. The notion that we should *just buy it*, rather than registering our intrinsic need over want, devalues us. And the truth is, they make the clothing because they know that, if it can be pushed on us in the right way, we'll buy it because we see more value in it than we do in ourselves. So how do we take our power back?

It's really simpler than you think: Buy less, buy *only* what you need, and separate needs from wants.

FACTORY SETTINGS

In order to keep up with the fast consumption cycle they have built, brands have to create a *lot* and they have to create it *very quickly*. When we buy things in large amounts or in bulk, the price automatically goes down. That's how our economy has always worked. The more you buy, the cheaper the overall price becomes, because the only way things become less valuable is if you buy *more* of them.

When a store is placing an order with a factory, the bigger the order, the lower the individual price of the pieces overall because…scale is leverage. You don't just see it in factories, you see it on websites like eBay, where an item is listed but if you buy two it gets cheaper, and if you buy three, wait for it, yup, it drops in price even further. And this reductive pricing filters down and down until it eventually reaches the bottom of the fashion and garment industry. Buyers from brands haggling with factories to get the lowest price possible for the goods being produced, which means the factory owner gets this chunk of money upon delivery to pay everyone out of, which sounds great, but it isn't a sustainable chain. Here's why:

As the order grows and grows, the supplier knows it will be harder and harder to fulfill. The brand also knows it will be hard to deliver, due to the scale of production and their impossibly quick turnaround time...Both parties know there is a limit to the amount any factory system can produce, because all clothing is made by human hands (though fashion is moving closer to automation every day, which I think will be another disaster). So, whether the order is being made in a factory or on a sewing machine in someone's home, human hands are doing the work. It is humans who cut the fabric, and humans who work tirelessly at sewing machines. And humans can only work so fast.

So, the factory owner has to work their garment workers to the bone, night and day, in order to fulfill this massive order, because if it's not delivered on time the brand can choose to walk away, leaving them with all the clothes (the factory owners, more likely than not, have paid for the fabrics and materials up front). And the likelihood is that if they lose this brand's business, their own business will collapse, and therefore so will the garment workers' jobs. But no matter how much the workers work, they can't fulfill this order because it's too giant. So they are forced to call up someone else who owns and runs a factory. And they have to outsource part of their order to that factory for a smaller amount than the store is paying them per garment. This outsourcing makes the target more achievable, but there is no information nor time to find out whether this factory pays its workers or cares for them in any way. There is no sense of what their labor costs, only the price of the individual garment. So, when it comes out that this second factory actually did not pay its workers and used children to do the job under brutal and dangerous conditions, yes, the big brand can claim that they didn't know that outsourcing would happen, but they *did* know that asking their factory to deliver hundreds of thousands of pieces in an impossibly short turnaround was, well, impossible. And they *did* know that somewhere down the chain there would be a cost. A human one. The most vulnerable would be paid the lowest wage, so the brand could keep its turnover as high as possible.

Whoever holds the power in the situation gets to choose whether or not to accept the merchandise, because there are a lot of "non-binding" contracts going on. A binding contract is one that is recognized in a court of law. The brands that manufacture their clothing in countries such as India, China, Bangladesh, Ethiopia, the Philippines, Thailand, and Vietnam claim that they do it for altruistic reasons and that it isn't about accessing the lowest wage in the supply chain. Karl-Johan Persson, former CEO of H&M, said in a *Bloomberg* interview that he's worried about how changing consumer behavior will negatively impact "the elimination of poverty." And yet, as Elizabeth Segran in *Fast Company* magazine in 2019 argued, this obscures the fact that H&M favors cheap labor in developing countries rather than using their factories to be altruistic. But these markets remain unregulated, and the wages are low because the countries are cash-poor (India and China notwithstanding). There is no altruism in paying extremely low prices for a garment wholesale, which will make a hefty profit, while quietly overlooking the fact that this system keeps generations of laborers in destitute poverty and ill health. Every now and then the fashion industry applauds some piecemeal action that a bigger brand does in a country where they manufacture. But what we should really be asking is why that big brand's business isn't lifting the people in that country out of poverty? Why aren't the hefty profit margins being shared in the countries where many brands manufacture?

The #PayUp campaign was started by the Remake community of fashion lovers, women's rights advocates, and environmentalists in March 2020, when much of the world had gone into lockdown due to the COVID-19 pandemic. All stores were shut and everyone behind closed doors began to freak out about sales and employment, while at the same time a great many brands decided now would be a good time not to pay for the clothing they had ordered from factories, which resulted in factory workers not being paid and many losing their jobs. We heard about it happening in Bangladesh, Pakistan, and India, but it also happened in manufacturing hubs like Bulgaria (the coverage just wasn't there, and people were afraid to speak up out of fear that they'd lose clients, including luxury brands).

Because this system of outsourcing has little legality or contractual obligation to bind a brand/corporation into playing fairly, many corporations just assumed they could walk away and leave their factories with their garments, some made, all textiles bought, and even some mid-shipment. Now, the factory usually pays for the materials for the clothes up front, so the factory owners are already out of pocket at the start of the chain (they receive payment from companies once the clothes have arrived at their shipment destination), so in this case, not only are they in debt, they are also unable to clear that debt and pay for the costs of the factory, workers, and shipping, too. A year on, in March 2021, Alison Morse reported on the Remake website that many brands still haven't paid their bills and are using this situation as a point of leverage to renegotiate with factories for more favorable prices wholesale—exploiting people at their most desperate. In addition, many brands have demanded discounts on their payments to their suppliers, relying on the *force majeure* clause in their contracts to shed responsibility for any financial loss incurred. How can this happen? Because there's no safety net for the world's most vulnerable people.

The system of outsourcing labor overseas for lower prices has similarities to the gig economy, which I saw sweep into the job market shortly after I graduated from university. In my lifetime, I've seen full-time jobs in many fields become contract work and zero-hour. Where our parents' generation had the option of working full-time in a slew of industries ("I just want to say one word to you: plastics"— *The Graduate*), we simply didn't have as many options if we wanted to be salaried. Why do big companies do this? Easy! It's cost-effective. I've never had a full-time, salaried job in my working life. And at one point in time, I wanted that *most*. That means I've also never worked for a company that has offered me health insurance, sick days, paid time off, or vacation time. For many years until the Affordable Care Act was passed, I was one of the millions of uninsured Americans (which means that if I got sick or broke a bone without insurance, I may have spent the rest of my life in medical debt).

When you make full-time positions freelance positions, you're ultimately paying less as a company (even if you have to pay a freelancer a better day rate than you pay your employees daily), because you as a corporation aren't paying for all those other things, which I would argue are definitely human rights. And when you outsource your labor jobs to another country because labor is cheaper there (due to years of exploitation and extraction), you're skimping on fair payment as well as all the things I listed above, not to mention safe working conditions.

It's much easier to get rid of a freelancer, whether you are in the legislated world or the unlegislated one. There are very few safety nets in place when a company chooses to terminate a contract for whatever reason. Or in the TV world...they just don't call you again. Been there, done that. It's always fun, that moment where you're not even sure what you did in particular, and they didn't even so much as write you a goodbye email (looking at a few previous employers here, and you know who you are if you're reading this book). I can only imagine how garment workers, factory owners, and those with far less than myself feel when this happens...every week. People who are below the poverty line, and therefore below human decency.

There is always a human cost.

I spoke to Anannya Bhattacharjee, international coordinator of Asia Floor Wage Alliance, which was formed as a Global South lead from Asia to bring a labor and social alliance between garment producing countries and consumer regions to address poverty-level wages, gender discrimination, and freedom of association in garment production networks. Bhattacharjee told me,

Colonized countries became politically independent when they brought their own government systems into existence expecting freedom. But what has really changed in the world today is the growth and the power, or capital, and that of Global North capital which is essentially global companies or multinational companies (some of whom have more power than whole countries). We are now living through a time when the power of capital embodied in these multinational companies is all powerful and they definitely dictate the conditions in the developing countries. Partly because there is a global belief about what a development model should look like—it is about the growth of capital, acquisition, and extraction, rather than distribution and regeneration and all that. So, the multinational Global North dictates the types of conditions that workers in the developing countries should have or the types of laws there should be on environmental regulation.

What should be happening is that the resources of that country should be regulated in the interests of amassing profits to multinational companies. Instead, what is actually happening is extraction; the multinationals are extracting the most profits for themselves, so although the workers in developing countries do get jobs, there is no talk put into what kind of jobs these are. These are jobs which are really robbing workers of their humanity, dignity, decency, they're going into debt. What we have is a very impoverished workforce, and the profits really end up in the hands of the multinationals, which only really enrich them and their home countries. So, when we think back to the model of colonialism, which is really extracting value and then taking that value to the colonizing, then this model continues today. But the agents of that have changed. The form has changed.

Because of the good work that activists in consumer countries have done, there is now some information out there about the lives of the workers who produce this clothing. Every consumer has the right to know under what conditions an item was made—be it labor conditions, environmental conditions—just like ingredients written on food packaging. It should also contain what the other hazards are that lie behind the product—the living and the dangerous and subhuman living and working conditions of the workers—what has gone into buying this piece of clothing at the price it is being sold for. A garment piece is often being sold at a price that does not reflect the cost of production and therefore it hides within it certain hazards. It's really important for consumers to know the conditions under which that piece of clothing was made. If they wear that piece of clothing, they should know that they are wearing something which conceals hazardous conditions that were necessary to produce it at the price paid for it.

> "What we need is a system of production and consumption that is attentive to what we need for our sustainable lives and for the planet."

Fast fashion is not just demeaning workers' lives, but destroying the planet because of its overconsumption of water and the destruction of oceans with microfibers. So, what we need is a system of production and consumption that is attentive to what we need for our sustainable lives and for the planet. Companies still need to make a profit, but we are currently operating at an extreme greed level—we need a much more balanced approach where people and planet are prioritized and companies can make a profit, but with a focus on regeneration, redistribution, and the balanced planet.

THE RACE TO THE BOTTOM

When people refer to our fashion production as it currently stands, you often hear the phrase "race to the bottom." The race to the bottom forces factories to compete against one another, quoting lower and lower prices (racing to the bottom), in order to win the much-needed contract. The race to the bottom also refers to high production targets (we're talking millions of the same product; that's what your orders sometimes look like when you have thousands of stores to stock), for cheap labor cost (the bigger the order, the more brands want discounted from the overall price per garment, which can often take your manufacturing cost pretty low...let's say £3 [and likely equivalent in the US] per garment, which is tricky and technically challenging to make), on a quick turnaround time. Ever wonder how stores manage to get new garments into the store every single day? It's the race to the bottom!

When you ask for less and less, who do you think pays for that? The factory? The garment workers? Both?

Anannya Bhattacharjee talks about this on the *Remember Who Made Them* podcast, saying, "So a garment worker who is getting paid usually the minimum wage really needs to get paid the living wage, and the gap is three times. What we want brands to pay is the gap between the minimum wage and the living wage. The supply factories are already paying the minimum wage, but the brands pay such a low price for the products to the supply factories that that price does not accommodate [a] living wage. Brands pay only for minimum wage and we believe that is not acceptable, given that this is such a high-revenue industry and the brands make a lot of profit."

Can you see how this sort of system traps factories and garment workers in a cycle that's nearly impossible to climb out of? Oh, and by the way, if the factory can't fulfill the order on time, there are very few legal rights that they have against big brands.

A brand can simply choose not to pay. Or, if you tell a brand, "No way, we're not going to do this for such a low price! That's insulting." Well then, they just take all their business away, leaving you with no work and facing factory closure. Just as small brands operate on small margins, so too do factories. Additionally, since factories often foot the bill for all the materials that go into the garment and only receive payment upon delivery of the goods, the factories are out of pocket and often with very little guarantee of any payment at all.

THE MATERIALS ECONOMY

The Story of Stuff is a short animated film, based on the book of the same name, available to view on YouTube that tells the story of the materials economy. What is the "materials economy"? It's our most dominant manufacturing system. The first stage is extraction and processing of raw materials. The second stage is factory production using the refined materials. The third and fourth stages are distribution of the manufactured products either to retail outlets or direct to consumers. The fifth stage is disposal.

The Story of Stuff focuses on the fact that you cannot run a linear system on a finite planet. What is a linear system? It's a straight line: materials—to consumer—to landfill. But you cannot have endless production on a finite planet. What that means is that our planet has limited resources, which we're all supposed to share. And they're quickly running out. An alternative is the circular system, which refers to no landfill and no end. Now, of course you'll probably think about how your favorite fast fashion brands have grand ideas of creating circular systems...in the future. But we need those systems today, and what we need most from these brands is for them to consider their scale...which in my mind is the biggest part of the problem. For example, you cannot have nearly 5,000 stores globally, which are stocked with new goods every single day, and claim that you're becoming "more sustainable." True sustainability requires less. And circular systems still require water and energy and extraction of resources and human labor.

Anannya Bhattacharjee says, "It's not just a labor demand, it's really for the planet, and we are in solidarity with the climate justice movement. The garment industry is very wasteful and is really destroying the planet, and fast fashion relies on overproduction and overconsumption. This model of operation is destroying our planet."

All of this will require fewer seasons. Seasons refers to every time a new set of garments arrives on a shop's floor. Some brands operate on fifty seasons a year—that's right, new clothes pretty much every week, and if they stagger it, that's new clothes being presented *every day*. And ultimately it will require *brands* to pay more money for the clothing that's being produced. Less clothing. More money for the workers. Less profit for the billionaires at top.

> "We need a cultural shift in how we view consumption."

We need a cultural shift in how we view consumption, as well as government regulation, because in many cases corporations can be bigger and more powerful than governments. In 2016, the online platform From Poverty to Power found that of the top one hundred economies on Earth, thirty-one were countries, sixty-nine were corporations. Starting to feel a bit ill at ease yet? Me too!

In 2018, Global Justice Now found that of the top wealthiest 200 economic entities, 157 were corporations. "Walmart, Apple, and Shell all accrued more wealth than even fairly rich countries like Russia, Belgium, Sweden." When we look at how we get to a solution, it becomes increasingly clear that it's going to take educating the consumer so that they demand better from the corporations before any government will begin to regulate these industries.

BUT ISN'T A JOB BETTER THAN NO JOB?

The simple answer is no.

The long answer is: these jobs are not better than nothing, because before we installed these systems, many of these countries were thriving in their own way. Don't forget, before colonialist rule, India was known for its fabric production. British colonialism actively disrupted that economy and began to trade off the back of it. Indigo from the Gold Coast was sought after by early European traders, who exploited natural resources for their own wealth accumulation. These places have always had the resources to thrive, and certainly the labor, but an uneven playing field has made it appear as though "they need us," whereas we built this whole thing off the backs of them. There is nothing fair and equitable about pilfering and exploitation. What would be fair is fair prices, fair wages, and evenly shared power. We need to do things better; we need to make these jobs and industries fairer and more equitable. We cannot continue to uphold castles made from dung and call it "better than nothing."

It is important also to note that there are actual clothing companies that manufacture overseas that do *not* exploit the people making their product. Plenty, actually. Despite what we've been led to believe about the free market, not everyone participates in the race to the bottom. That's something that multinational corporations (and a few others) choose to do. It's an active choice by those who hold the most amount of power; no one's hands are tied here. There are fashion brands that actually make the members of the supply chain *employees* of their company. Meaning, there are perks like paid time off. Sick days. Basic human rights. There's employer responsibility. And there are also clothing brands that are beginning to move back into the direction of owning their own factories and having an actual stake in their production. There are many ways to make clothing, domestically and internationally, that do not involve exploiting people. I suggest we champion those ways.

> "There are many ways to make clothing, domestically and internationally, that do not involve exploiting people."

Next time someone says, "Well, at least those people have a job," remember this one fact: increasing the price of a garment in the shop by 1 percent could be enough to pay the workers who made it a living wage. This was forecasted by a Deloitte Access Economics report in 2017 on costing the impact of a living wage in Australia's supply chain.

Remember that there are billionaires at the top of so many of these multinational corporate fashion brands. Is there really any excuse for those at the bottom to be living in such abject poverty?

The idea that these countries need us to be in charge in order to ensure they have profitable and successful economies is a hangover from colonialism that we need to interrogate. Certain countries have been "in charge" for a while, and the world is in a whole-ass mess.

If everyone has to play by the same rules, and those rules uphold human rights, none of us has to worry about whether or not that t-shirt we've bought has caused more human strife. I'd rather fight for that than waste a second of my life defending a system that is still actively and knowingly exploiting others for financial gain.

THE SCARCITY MODEL

You can't globalize *and also* create scarcity.

The entire scarcity model and mentality of brands make me feel deeply uncomfortable, and should make you feel the same way, because wealth inequality is at its widest gap ever. I'm of the belief that there would be plenty for everyone if the few didn't take much more than their fair share. And that's part of why I'm not big on the fast fashion brands. Producing millions of garments for a percentage of the planet (bearing in mind that most garment workers cannot afford the clothing they produce), which then get incinerated every year (because that's how fast the cycle goes, in order to keep up the scarcity model), aids and fuels poverty but uses the valuable resources on Earth that we're all supposed to share. How is that right?

Here's an example, as quoted on the *No Such Thing as a Fish* podcast: American caviar used to be exported to Europe, repackaged as Russian, and then imported back to America to be sold at a higher price. Why? Because of the scarcity economic model and the idea that Russian caviar was billed as superior when, it's pretty clear, many could not taste the difference.

A Note on How Much "It" Is Worth

What was the "It" bag? It was a bag that had been seen on a minimum of three celebrities at a time, often because the brand had gifted those celebrities that bag, and the celebrities had considered the bag worthy of being carried. I first began to notice the popularity of certain bags when I lived in London. At the time, though, I didn't have the wherewithal to recognize how once again my longing to be accepted was powering my desire to engage in conspicuous consumption. I just thought I really, really, really wanted *that* bag! And *that* bag! And in another year or two *that* bag, too.

Handbags are big business for brands. Grand View Research reported in 2019 that the global handbag market is expected to grow at a compound annual growth rate of 5.4 percent from 2019 to reach US$67.85 billion by 2025.

The bags have a fairly low overhead when you consider production and materials, but the mark-up has always been the stuff that keeps brands afloat. Plus, it's a great way for many brands to continue to be fatphobic and not make more sizes. As they sure will sell you an accessory so you too can feel like you're a part of the "dream," while being completely excluded from it. I think once that dawned on me, I was truly cured of "It" bags personally. Because I find it nauseating.

Later I would realize, with the "It" bags I had managed to obtain with my hard-won dollars, that white people would always casually ask me if my bag was "real." I mean what is even the point in having the bag if people assume it's fake anyway because you're Black? (For the record, I have never carried, and will never carry, a fake handbag. I'd rather not have one at all than fuel that problematic and exploitative market.) But racism really knows how to take the air out of your tires. But in a way of turning lemons into lemonade, I do think those sort of rude and racist assumptions finally helped me to wise up to the ridiculous merry-go-round I was riding.

I had seen at least ten "It" bags come and go before I began to realize...this is a con.

But even the tote bag trend was still driven by manufactured frenzy and desire. Does anyone remember the Anya Hindmarch I Am Not A Plastic Bag? I do! The bags, which were launched in 2007 to encourage shoppers to start thinking about moving away from plastic bags for purchases, created legit hype once they were spotted on a slew of celebrities. At the time I was residing in New York City, where I was focused on getting a degree in learning about privilege, extreme nepotism, unpaid labor, and all the terrible practices that the magazine industry continues to perpetuate. On the day of the launch I thought I'd just mosey down to the store (located conveniently across the street from the magazine) and pick up one of the £5 ($10 in the US) bags for myself. No such luck. By the time the store opened, the lines for the bags had wrapped around the block on Greene Street. So, even in a world where we recognize the need to move away from plastic bags and have a moment to have a real conversation... fashion managed to turn it into an absolute frenzy of conspicuous consumption. Today you can buy one of the famous bags on eBay for £150 ($120 US). Nice.

The I Am Not A Plastic Bag trend would have made BIPOC parents and grandparents everywhere roll their eyes in deep frustration. Same for poor people (including poor white folks). Because truthfully you can use *any* bag to put your groceries in, and those without have been doing that...all along. And, of course, reusing plastic bags, too.

One brand I saw rise to prominence while spending time in London was Orla Kiely. The cool London girls loved Orla Kiely circa 2003, so naturally...I loved Orla Kiely, too. To be fair, I'm a real sucker for a mod print any given day. The first time I came across one of the bags, the price tag made me wince (champagne tastes on beer money in 2003). However, when I moved back to the US, I was excited to see the bags make an appearance at Anthropologie, and the exchange rate actually worked in my favor, so I bought one. But they didn't exactly fly off the shelves, because the trend cycle hadn't signified to the US that this was "the thing to have" just yet.

A year or two later I was up in New York for work. I was walking back to my sister's fifth-story walk-up apartment when I diverted into an Anthropologie on my walk home. I immediately headed to the sale room (because why wouldn't you when there's always stuff marked down). To my surprise the store's entire stock of Orla Kiely bags had been marked down to more than half off. They were positively inexpensive. Suddenly the wheels in my head began to turn. I knew the brand had been popular, but I didn't understand why no one had wanted to buy these bags. I knew someone elsewhere would want them all. Before I fully understood what I was doing, I was marching to the register with an armful of twenty-five handbags.

("Hold up, wait a minute" [I've borrowed that directly from the *Politically Re-Active* podcast with W. Kamau Bell and Hari

Kondabolu; they're great!]: Here's where we talk about priv-ilege. At this moment I had the absolute privilege of a good credit score. A person living paycheck to paycheck couldn't just decide to spend $400 on bags in one shot. This is where we take the hashtag #GirlBoss right out of the story. I'm not some sort of boss because I had the privilege of a good credit score and not living paycheck to paycheck. But I could do it because my credit's always been good, because I come from a stable two-parent home with two adults who taught me a little bit about financial literacy from a young age. These things *absolutely* mat-ter. If your parents don't understand the ways in which finan-cial systems work, there's a very good chance you won't either. When credit card companies started sending me credit cards at a really young age, my mother would shred them before I even got home from school. And she saved me by doing that, because I surely would have made a mess of it. But I also knew that if I didn't sell the bags, I could at least return them. What an odd return that would be. Put another way, I didn't have to choose between buying groceries or $400 worth of designer bags.)

When I got to my sister's house, she looked at me like I had finally "done it" this time. Semi-disgust, semi-confusion (because I was fairly broke at the time; I was sleeping on her sofa). "Don't worry, I'm going to sell them all!" I hollered as I headed to the door, jacket and purse in hands. My next stop was down to a bodega to buy two of those plaid carrier bags to carry them all in. You know, the ones that high-end designers ripped off, art mimicking life and all that. You see, I was planning to ride the Chinatown Dragon Coach from NYC back to DC, and I couldn't take five massive shopping bags on a bus. I managed to fold and neatly cram all of my bounty into the carrier bags and arrive at the bus with my luggage and two additional bags slung over my shoulders.

When my dad greeted me from the other side in DC, standing outside his black car, he watched me unloading my bags from the storage compartment of the bus and became more and more confused.

"Don't worry, I'm gonna sell them all!" I said.

Slowly but surely, listing each bag on eBay, I was able to sell every bag I had purchased for sometimes four times more than I had actually paid for it. My parents watched dumbfounded as they slowly disappeared from the basement. Not bad for a girl from Virginia who always knew the cost of living.

The point here is that goods have a fluctuating price depending on the market *and* the demand. If there's too much of something in a place where there isn't the demand, then those goods will lose their value. Demand is essentially an artificial creation. Everything is essentially valueless if it's in the wrong place at the wrong time.

In order to keep prices for premium goods at a premium level, the buyer has to buy into the fact that the product they are consuming is in scarce supply in the production chain and is not available to buy en masse. This gives the product a rarity that not only keeps the price stable but also can increase it.

When brands burn their inventory, they're doing two things.

1. They're being incredibly wasteful. Don't create things if you're just going to incinerate them once they have reached their sell-by date, aka you don't want to pay to store them in warehouses. That's cotton that didn't have to be grown, wool which didn't have to be sheared, leather which didn't have to be produced, water used in all processes down the drain… so, what, you can look cool and lie about how much you're producing?

2. They're pushing fraudulent claims. There is a scarcity mentality of pushing products that rapidly turn over, making you think that you need to rush out early and often to see "what's new?" in store. There's a sense of urgency in the email spam you receive in your inbox, encouraging you to shop daily and often with coupons and language such as "don't miss out."

Why not create better-quality clothes that have a longer life, instead of wasting the resources we have on a planet that is stretched to the brink of disaster?

5

HOW SOCIETY WORKS

In some ways we're lucky to live in "this time." Rachel Ricketts believes that we all chose to be here for this time right now, on this planet—predestined, more or less. I kind of believe that myself, and then sometimes I think, *Oh goodness no, surely there were better times to be alive and Black*...though that's debatable in recent history. This is our time. One of the main things that I do consider as being lucky about existing at this time on Earth is that we have the framework of intersectionality.

WHAT IS INTERSECTIONALITY AND WHY DO WE NEED IT?

Intersectionality is the framework I use when looking at many of our societal issues, and I strongly believe it applies to the fashion supply chain conversation, too. Developed by Kimberlé Crenshaw in 1989, the concept of intersectionality has quickly become a household phrase. In an interview with Katy Steinmetz for *Time* magazine in 2020, Crenshaw explained that intersectionality is "basically a lens, a prism, for seeing the way in which various forms of inequality often operate together and exacerbate each other. We tend to talk about race inequality as separate from inequality based on gender, class, sexuality, or immigrant status. What's often missing is how some people are subject to all of these, and the experience is not just the sum of its parts."

Why is it important for this conversation? If we look at multiple intersections of the supply chain, then we begin to see the oppressions in a more effective way, as we view them all together rather than in silo. We start to understand why the people on the bottom of the supply chain have always been there, and why those at the top have always been there. For instance, garment workers live in poverty because of the low wages they are paid, and then we can also take into account that most garment workers are women, and with that also comes further income inequality. As Crenshaw has explained: "Numerous statistics show that women still get paid less for the same work. That multiplies over a lifetime and means that the problem gets worse the older women get. There's also a term called the feminization of poverty, which speaks to all the ways that life circumstances—like child rearing, divorce, illness—impact women more profoundly." And now let's take into account the garment workers' BIPOC identities. "When you add on top of that other inequality-producing structures like race, you have a compounding. So for example, data show that white women's median wealth is somewhere in the $40,000 range. Black women's is $100."

When we look at all intersections, we begin to understand why the system has such control over those at the bottom. It actively preys on the most marginalized and powerless.

What I return to time and time again is how the world we live in has prospered off breaking the backs of people. But *it is these people* that live in a way that we should have...this whole time.

To solve the problems of the world, you're going to have to start listening and decentering white voices—whether it's listening to those who make the products you buy, or those who protect the Amazon as powerful corporations make moves to destroy it, or indeed those who protect the water on the lands we all share, or those who are left at the end of your supply chain cleaning up the mess. Educator, activist, and founding director of the Land Peace Foundation Sherri Mitchell Weh'na Ha'mu Kwasset, Penawahpskek Nation, has pointed out: "Those who once claimed that Indigenous issues were fringe or ephemeral are now recognizing that protecting Indigenous rights is an ecological necessity."

> "You're going to have to start listening to those who are most oppressed."

You're going to have to start listening to those who are most oppressed. We might not have all the power (because if we did things would look different), but we have the knowledge. Especially when it comes to collective organizing, and when it comes to protecting and maintaining environments. Every time I attend a meeting in a majority-white space about organizing, I find that white people without irony reference movements led by marginalized BIPOC people, for example Martin Luther King Jr. and civil rights. So why is *everyone* on the stage white? I know people say, "We are listening," but how can you when so many of our stories have been written out of history, so you can't find them to listen to? The knowledge has always been there...It just depends on who you're willing to receive it from. And that's going to require a lot of unpacking.

I read the article "Indigenous Prophecy and Mother Earth" by Sherri Mitchell Weh'na Ha'mu Kwasset in the book *All We Can Save*, which made me think about the interconnectedness of all of us: "Indigenous knowledge recognizes the individuality of elements in the natural world and how they relate to a larger whole using traditional family kinship models as their scaffold. It does this without stripping away the individual value or attempting to form what is being seen into a larger body of generalized laws or theories. It simply recognizes the familial relationship and acknowledges that all life is both sovereign and interdependent, and that each element within creation (including humans) has the right and the responsibility to respectfully coexist as coequals within the larger system of life."

In the words of Dr. Ayana Elizabeth Johnson: "We are all connected and so I think the sooner people realize that, the better we will all be."

I couldn't agree more.

WHY THE GENDER BINARY IS MESSING IT UP

If your feminism is intersectional, then you should be including *everyone* in it: men, women, trans people, non-binary people, and every gender. At the very least, anyone should be able to walk into any store and buy whatever garment they want, with nary a question or second look.

As Wikipedia defines it: "The term *gender binary* describes the system in which a society allocates its members into one of two sets of gender roles, gender identities, and attributes based on the type of genitalia."

The gender binary therefore insists that all people are defined by one of two boxes, regardless of whether you want to be in that box or whether or not either of those boxes holds your identity. It enforces roles in society based on what's between your legs. This determines how you should behave and where there is space for you in our society. It is oppressive and it is harmful. Ever heard of the pink tax? Basically "women's" stuff often costs more, for God knows what reason. Clothing, hygiene products, shoes, you name it. That's the gender binary hard at work.

Why are we categorized before we even decide who we want to be? Why are some categories more powerful than others?

Guess what also sailed in on the fleet of colonial ships...the model of *gender binary. Another crappy import.* People of various genders have existed since the beginning of humanity. Other cultures know and recognize this, but around five hundred years ago the few began to restrict the masses by categorization. This happened to Indigenous people of the colonized states of America. To India. To the Aboriginal people. In Mali, Ghana, Burkino Faso, the Ivory Coast, Hawaii. The Incans. Did all this change with colonialism? Why, yes, it did!

As a matter of fact, PBS's "The Origin of Gender" from the *Origin of Everything* history series makes a very interesting link, as host Professor Danielle Bainbridge says: "It comes as no surprise then that with the rise of colonization which often looked to regulate and standardize farming practices across different regions that we also see a solidification of gender roles becoming the norm. This is also coupled with the fact that often people in colonized regions were severely punished for expressing any gender, sex, or sexual expression outside of the accepted norm of two genders and two sexes."

Many societies operated just fine without these rules until oppressive powers told everyone how you were supposed to exist...and now we're supposed to live like this forever. Nah! Miss me out on that.

Not only is the gender binary harming anyone who doesn't fit neatly into the box of "defined gender," but it's ultimately harming cis women, too. I have often used the colloquialism "women be shopping," but if we peer beneath this supposed "female pastime" and pull back the layers, this concept of women as shoppers has for time immemorial been planted as what we do best as an activity. In times and places where gender roles were even more strictly codified, it *was* women who did the shopping, and who enjoyed the independence of making their own decisions, carrying out canny purchasing, and fulfilling this extension of care-giving. You should enjoy shopping, for god's sake! You're a woman after all! This is what you are good for!

This is pounded into our heads from pretty early on, and of course that identity comes with a slew of insecurities fueled by us being inundated with marketing on what makes the perfect woman. Advertising geared toward women is big money. You need a new lipstick! You need new workout clothes! You can't wear the same dress to a wedding! Gotta get a new one even if you don't feel like it. Gotta be a better version of yourself if you want to be happy and accepted or loved.

A Note on Men and Women Shopping for Special Occasions

Wedding dress shopping was absolute hell for me. Not only did I have teeny tiny sizes to contend with (once you get past a US size 12, your choices radically drop off a cliff), but it was such incredible stress to get it perfect. Meanwhile, wanna know what my partner did? He went into his wardrobe, pulled out a suit he had had made on his travels, dusted it off, and said he was good to go. I've never been so envious of my significant other in my life. Here I was, pulling out my hair because let's put the narrative of "one perfect day" into girls' heads from a young age and this slacker over here wears the same suit he always wears? Are you kidding me?

The gender binary plants pretty harmful narratives into our heads from a very young age about what sort of treatment we should expect from society and how we should behave. How we should dress according to our femininity or masculinity (which leaves, of course, no room for anyone else in between). And let's not even go there with the notion that women should power-dress in men's clothes. What does that say to a young woman? That in order to be powerful you have to play like the boys! While still being feminine, of course! But, wait, where does everyone else fit?

Now, imagine if that one day—poof—it went away. Imagine how free we'd all feel?

I think we would feel liberated. And free to dress in a way that allowed us to express who we really are, not who we have been told to be, or who we think we should be.

HOW EVERYBODY IS CONNECTED

There's a popular phrase I see uttered on Twitter. And it is so simple, yet so poignant and true.

"I don't know how to make you care about other people."

(It breaks my heart every time I read it.)

There's a real disconnect happening with us and our clothes, and that's perhaps because the person who makes our clothes lives far away in a country we haven't visited or know relatively little about. That tricky cognitive dissonance between what you buy and the system you are supporting by putting your money there isn't easily connected unless you put the time into joining up the dots that link you back to the person hand-sewing your jeans.

Indeed, there is even this societal myth that these people in remote lands from us should be "happy" for a wage that doesn't feed them or their children, that the person sorting through piles of leftover fashion in their backyard should feel "lucky" that we "donated" our goods in their direction (ignoring the real ecological crisis caused by said actions). Perhaps we care less because we can't see ourselves in any of these people? It's much easier when it translates to your own life, your backyard, your wage. Let's just be honest. We buy and donate clothing because there's this little voice that tells us that we're being saviors to someone who is otherwise without resources, while ignoring the simple facts that these actions ultimately aid more in oppression than anything else.

This makes me think of NIMBY, which stands for Not In My Back Yard. Liz Ricketts uses NIMBY in her talks about Kantamanto Market: "Landfill development is a prime example, one that served as the foundation of Dr. Robert Bullard's brave environmental justice work. For many privileged people, often white people in the Global North, waste is out of sight, out of mind, because this waste is often being displaced from affluent white neighborhoods to predominantly Black and POC neighborhoods. NIMBY isn't always racial, because poor white people can find themselves with landfill waste sitting next to their neighborhoods, too, but it certainly shows up in the secondhand clothing trade." As Ricketts suggests, perhaps it is the "manifestation of the ignorance made possible by white supremacist ideologies and segregation."

"Fundamentally," Liz says, "NIMBYism is the idea that something isn't good enough for me, but it will be fine for you. That is the definition of supremacism. To think that 'I won't wear this because there is a hole in it, but someone else can wear it,' is literally to think that I am better than someone else, even if the impulse to give something away is filled with good intentions. Whatever the declared intentions, the NIMBY attitude manifests further injustice."

The truth is...it is all connected.

We are all connected on this planet.

And not just in a trite, ignorant, "I-don't-see-color" way.

(If you don't know why "I don't see color" doesn't exactly reassure your BIPOC friends, there are a lot of resources on Google about that one. Blackness is a part of my identity. I'm okay with it. Why aren't you?)

133

More so in the fact that the dye that pollutes that water stream will find a way into yours sooner or later. Or in the way the microplastics that shed off of all polyester fibers can find a way into the water system through washing. (If you are a pregnant person they may even find their way into your placenta.)

You should care about these systems because you *care about people*, and how you consume affects a lot of people. Author and garment-industry journalist Tansy Hoskins writes: "Young people in Britain taking on debt to buy clothes is mirrored by people in the Global South being forced into debt in order to produce fashion." If you were the person at the Global South end of the power spectrum, wouldn't you wish that the people consuming the goods that you were never able to (and that they can't afford either), the same goods that destroyed your planet, wouldn't you want them to care a little bit more, too?

Don't lean into the unseen areas for safety. Step out of them in order to see the lives of others more clearly and to realize we are all connected. You and me. Even though it's just words connecting us right now, we are in conversation and you can hear me (although I may never hear you). Every cause has an effect. Every word can bring about change. Every decision can be a step forward. You should care about the people you can't see or don't know, and who may never see or know you, because these same toxic systems are coming for you, too. It may take longer, but it eventually will harm us all.

And all you'll have to show for it is a pile of stuff.

6

CULTURAL APPROPRIATION

A quick disclaimer before I begin this chapter: I, Aja Barber, can only speak from my experience on this subject as a Black person. Black people are not a monolith. There are many experiences out there, but this is mine and mine alone. So often people tie themselves in knots over this subject because they feel a particular ownership to something which isn't of their culture and don't want it stripped from them—even though it wasn't theirs in the first place. And this is where the harm is really done, and it's apparent in all of our Westernized culture.

Still unclear on it?

Okay.

Let's break it down.

Say you have two teams, a blue team and a green team. Each team has their own ball, blue and green respectively. The blue team already has an advantage in the game as they have more players; on top of that, an invisible referee takes away the green team's ball and tells them they can only participate if they play with the blue ball, which disadvantages them further. Three quarters of the way through the match, the invisible referee gives the blue team their blue ball *and* the green ball, and everyone admires how the blue team plays with both balls. When the green team balks at this, the blue team asks them why they're being spoilsports and why everyone can't play with everyone's balls. (Yes, pun intended. Yes, I am laughing at my joke because I'm immature.) The green team is declared spoilsports, and the blue team is declared the winner and the most graceful, despite having had clear and obvious advantages repeatedly handed to them in the game.

This is why it doesn't work when a white person who likes locs or box braids gets annoyed because Black people have chemically straightened their hair. Do you think if given a choice every Black person who has straightened their hair would have chosen that path? I think not. Some would and that's okay and not anyone's business to critique until we fully critique white supremacy and colonization. This is the result of living in a society where your own hair, culture, style of dress, and clothing are demonized, and in order to get ahead you have to shed the parts of you that are a part of your identity in order to be more fit for consumption.

This is a toxic disadvantage, one that is all too invisible in the world because the powerful decide the rules. The biased rules mean they will always, always win.

DON'T TOUCH THE HAIR

As a person who suffers from uterine fibroids, I see how history and cultural oppression has harmed Black people like myself.

According to a 2012 article in *Essence* magazine, "A new study published in the *American Journal of Epidemiology* reports that the use of hair relaxers may increase the risk of uterine fibroids." If that isn't enough, the article goes on to say, "Black women had reportedly two or three times higher rate of uterine fibroids."

I hate my fibroids and wish I could go back in time and *never* chemically straighten my hair (because I didn't exactly enjoy the process of hair straightening—it was painful and costly and each hair appointment lost me precious hours of living my life...no ten-year-old wants to sit in a salon chair for more than an hour). But I would have been teased at school for my "different" hair (although, let's face it, I was teased even when it *was* straightened) and possibly demonized in the workplace, so I totally understand why I did it and other people do, too; we want to do all we can to not make our lives any harder.

A polite note to the white folks: hair is a touchy topic, whether it's natural or straightened. It's not really your business to comment or insist you like it one way or another, and please, for the love of all things holy, *don't touch the hair.* I mean Solange had to *write a song about it.* That's how bad things have gotten. As of 2019, in the US, you still have laws being overturned in regard to hairstyle and what is considered "professional" in the workplace. These laws were created to be oppressive to people from marginalized identities because their identities were not respected or tolerated by the people in power. They were deemed outside of the rules.

Continuing on the subject of hair touching, author Isabel Wilkerson writes about this in her seminal work, *Caste.* She says, "If there is anything that distinguishes caste, however, it is, first, the policing of roles and behavior expected of people based on what they look like, and second, the monitoring of boundaries, the disregard for the boundaries of the subordinate caste, or the passionate construction of them by those of the dominant caste to keep the hierarchy in place."

The truth is, any white person I know would think it was weird if a total stranger just walked up to them and started touching their hair. And yet, that is my *reality*. It happens at least once a year, and the only reason I don't slap people is because I don't want to go to jail. There are enough Black people in the unjust prison system as it is.

Touching a stranger's hair is an act of utter disrespect for their humanity and boundaries. When you do it without absolute permission to a Black person, you're just playing into systems of racism that have existed for years, ones that tell you a Black person's body doesn't actually belong to them.

> "Touching a stranger's hair is an act of utter disrespect for their humanity and boundaries."

INDIGENOUS APPROPRIATION

As early as 1790 we have historical records that show the US banned indigenous artifacts as a way to oppress communities and their culture, which was done repeatedly throughout their colonized history.

There was an actual federal push for assimilation (yes, this was done by the government), and this push put North American Indigenous children in boarding schools where they were forbidden from using their own language, or practicing their religion and culture. These children were taken from their families, given new names, Anglicized names. Their hair was cut. Hair is sacred in many cultures. The damage from these actions still harms North American Indigenous communities today.

So, no, many Indigenous people don't want to see you prancing around in a headdress at a festival when their ancestors couldn't wear them because of colonialism.

In the US, Japanese artifacts were seized during World War II when many Japanese citizens were pushed into internment camps (despite the fact that the US didn't treat German and Italian citizens in the same manner during that time period). I now understand that calling any old dress or robe with a certain type of sleeve a "kimono" is really wrong and outdated. Kimonos are beautiful Japanese ceremonial garments, sometimes passed down through generations, and should be respected as such.

BENEATH THE SURFACE

You may be wondering why I'm including a chapter on cultural appropriation in a book about consumerism. Here it is: we have to be incredibly careful and vigilant because cultural appropriation can harm marginalized people on a deeper level. The concept of racial capitalism is one discussed first by professor Cedric Robinson and later by professor Nancy Leong. Racial capitalism focuses on the way in which brands extract monetary value from non-whiteness. Racial capitalism views diverse and marginalized identities as a commodity to be bought and sold. It's the reason all those black squares on Instagram looked like performative allyship at its finest: because racial capitalism is all about money and numbers and less about long-lasting change, allyship, and true positive change.

Some of the overlapping themes that exist within racial capitalism include virtue signaling, defensiveness in the conversation about racism and specifically using Black and brown bodies with ulterior motives in mind, and adopting their practices and culture to benefit your own perceived value.

INVESTIGATING RACIAL CAPITALISM

Let's go a little deeper down this rabbit hole and look at racial capitalism's proximity to cultural appropriation by looking at who is getting paid to present whose culture to the masses and who is not.

When a big brand that has ignored marginalized communities for decades, if not centuries, decides to jump on the "trend" of a cultural item (let's say indigenous-inspired garments or Black Lives Matter t-shirts), because of the bigger brands' proximity to whiteness, size, and power, they're going to receive positive press automatically for "taking up the cause," even if they're not doing the actual work within their organization and not giving up power to marginalized people within the communities they seek to capitalize on.

If a smaller designer within that community has been providing for that community all along but the bigger brand decides to give that designer "friendly competition," the smaller brand might be put out of business by the bigger, likely white-owned, company which is just trying to capitalize on an opportunity and not actually give back to that community. All of this matters in the game of who is allowed power, money, and control and who isn't. And then of course don't get me started on the countless times I've seen a brown or Black designer ripped off by the ultra-fast-fashion heavies. That seems to happen every other week (and is mostly my reason for keeping Twitter, because these cases always come across my timeline). At the time of my writing, Fisayo Longe, creative director of Kai Collective, is currently embroiled in a battle with Boohoo, who blatantly ripped off her beautiful designs.

> "All of this matters in the game of who is allowed power, money, and control and who isn't."

In a Buzzfeed article, Longe said, "I just think that it is so ethically wrong for them to use our ideas to build their own entire empires, they're using our ideas to build wealth, becoming billionaires, and then selling that back to us. That's just so dark to me." Longe also called on consumers to give more consideration to the brands they chose to support.

Granted, this happens to white independent designers, too, but the frequency with which certain mega brands target Black designers certainly isn't missed by me or anyone else keeping an eye out.

BLACKFISHING

And let me not forget cultural appropriation's younger, hipper Instagram-friendly sister, Blackfishing. Blackfishing is evident when someone who is frankly...white pretends that they aren't. It's Rachel Dolezal–ing for the social media world. Tools include bronzer, tanner, makeup, hair styling, sometimes wigs. It's the act of aiming for racial ambiguity (or just Blackness) when you're white. Why is it harmful? That again is another book of its own. To summarize it quickly, I would say because we know that most spaces pertaining to fashion and media hold whiteness as a barrier to entry, why are you pretending to be us when we're already locked out? If the world doesn't allow BIPOC to join these spaces without jumping through flaming hoops, it's rather frustrating and harmful to see white people swanning around pretending to be us. It's the modern-day form of a minstrel show (they were, and are, the worst. These types of shows were popular in the US in the 1900s, in which mostly white performers wore blackface and portrayed Black characters as lazy and boorish). Blackfishing is a perpetuation of not only *not* tearing down barriers but also mocking the very people you both consciously and unconsciously lock out.

LET'S CONSIDER CULTURAL APPRECIATION

Let's unpack the cultural appreciation argument alongside cultural appropriation. First, ask the question, do the people who belong to whatever culture you claim to be "appreciating" feel appreciated? If the answer is yes, that's great! If the answer is no, stop what you're doing at once. These conversations are nuanced and require a lot of listening and self-interrogation in order to do the right thing. You have to be prepared to do the work. If you're not prepared to listen, recognize that. Also, consider whether you are cherry-picking your most apolitical marginalized friend to ask them if it's "okay if you do this thing." If so, you likely aren't looking to have an honest conversation about why these things may be problematic. You are actually trying to make the problem go away. You are just searching for the same cognitive bias in order to absolve your problematic views or actions. Because, yes, marginalized people, just like white people, can be apolitical. That is a choice afforded to *everyone*. Sometimes carrying the weight of a marginalized identity is enough to make you want to shy away from any conversation about race and inequality. I know this because I lived my life that way for years, not wanting to have the conversation because I didn't want to carry the weight of my own identity, oppression, and white people's hurt feelings and fragility over learning about the ways their past actions may have harmed others. So I simply avoided talking about it. Marginalized people of all ethnicities get to be just like white people in the fact that some of us literally do not want to be involved. The struggle is real and lifelong, and sometimes it's too much to carry.

> "Sometimes carrying the weight of a marginalized identity is enough to make you want to shy away from any conversation about race and inequality."

Ultimately, it's a transparent way to avoid being challenged. It's almost as if you just want a Black person to agree with you so you can carry on doing your thing.

It's also worth mentioning at this juncture that, if you have a Black or brown friend who you know has opinions on race that they discuss in other areas of their life but never with you, take a moment, breathe, and realize that maybe you've not earned their trust. Maybe they don't want to discuss this topic with you because you've not done the work to show that you're someone who can be trusted with the conversation and who is willing to learn. Maybe you've been fragile with them in the past, so they clam up and can't be truly open with you. And whose fault is that?

HOLDING MY HAND UP

In the nineties, I began to realize that London might just be the place I wanted to spend a good portion of my adult life, mostly because all the music I loved was coming from the UK, and that's a great way to plan the rest of your life, right? A girl from Virginia who loves Bjork, Portishead, and the Sneaker Pimps can dream, right? However, the nineties were also *rife* with cultural appropriation; almost everyone was doing it. Even I can hold my hand up right here because of that t-shirt I had with the Hindu god on it, whose name I didn't even know but was still wearing like decoration—that was cultural appropriation.

Imagine a scene where two white girls are standing together and one is wearing t-shirt with an image of Jesus being crucified.

"Whoa, cool t-shirt, what does it mean?"

"I don't know! I just really liked the design!"

See? Awkward.

People were also getting lots of regrettable tattoos written in languages we didn't even speak because the script "looked cool."

I shudder to think about all the mistakes I myself almost made. But I'm also grateful to be better educated now. When we normalize changing our opinion when presented with new information, we allow everyone to move forward.

In the late nineties, I didn't have the language to discuss exactly why things didn't make sense to me. Why did the Indian and Pakistani girls in 1996 get othered in school for wearing bindis, but when a white pop star decided to wear them, they suddenly started appearing in fashion magazines adorning teenage celebrities for photo shoots? Why is it that Black and brown people aren't allowed to enjoy things from our actual culture until it becomes "fashion"? One day cornrows are considered "ghetto"; the next week they're on the runway. But Black people are still considered "ghetto" by the white masses when we wear them.

Once, on a call with a tech company, I was asked, "What is the difference between cultural appropriation and cultural appreciation?"

The answer to this is far easier than you think. It requires empathy, but turned right.

CULTURAL APPROPRIATION FAQ

A quick Q & A on cultural appropriation:

Q: I am going to a wedding in India. Is it appropriate to wear a sari?

A: Does your host think it's appropriate? Does their family think it's appropriate? Why not ask about the dress code (as you would for a wedding in the West)? I'm sure they're more than happy to share. If you have the pleasure of wearing a sari, respect it.

Q: I have this headdress. It's not quite Indigenous, but I can't figure out if it's inappropriate.

A: If you don't have any Indigenous friends to ask, you probably shouldn't be wearing anything vaguely Indigenous. Let's just say it's a no.

Q: Can white people wear #BlackLivesMatter shirts?

A: It's a toss-up, and I think a lot of Black people might not necessarily agree with me (as I mentioned earlier, we're not a monolith and we all disagree all the time). I'm fine with it under certain circumstances. Make sure you're buying that t-shirt from a Black-owned business (as white people should not be profiting off the Black Lives Matter movement in any way whatsoever). Make sure you're standing up for Black people in uncomfortable conversations, instead of just wearing a t-shirt. Ask yourself if you are prepared to have the uncomfortable conversations that probably shouldn't be uncomfortable at all. If so, that's great. Educate your fellow white people, if you're white.

Q: But my friend said it was okay.

A: Then why are you asking me? If you feel guilty or weird, maybe you should investigate that.

Do you notice that every time it's a question about a culture I don't belong to, I mention that you should ask your friend? If you don't have any friends from that culture, you should probably leave it alone. I can't speak for every marginalized group or culture, nor would I want to. If someone from a culture tells you that you're doing something harmful, it's always good to listen!

7

SHOPPING: THE GREAT CON

What do we mean when we talk about affordability? People constantly conflate the idea of affordability with the idea that no one is paying the price for the low, low, low prices at the checkout. You may be able to come up with the cash, but I'll tell you who can't afford this system. The farmers who grow the cotton can't afford this system. At the time of writing, there are farmer protests in India, which is the largest cotton producer in the world. Cotton farmers are notoriously ripped off, especially by the Global North. The problem is so pernicious that the rate of suicide in farmers is far higher than one would expect (according to the *Economic Times*, the suicide rate in India in 2019 for farmers and daily wagers was 42,480). Cotton farming and practices is a dirty business.

Affordability it ain't for the garment workers. Most garment workers cannot afford to buy the clothes they make.

Is it affordable for the upcyclers of Kantamanto Market, who are tasked with disposing of our waste?

Please stop referring to this system as affordable.

The planet cannot afford the environmental costs, and neither can most of its inhabitants.

The truth is that too many of us are buying too much because our bank accounts and credit cards mean we can afford to.

But can we?

I remember when we paid more for our clothes...and if you're older than thirty you probably remember, too. Especially if you were forced to know the cost of items because you did not have extreme financial privilege.

Around eleven, I started having fights with my mother about clothes, particularly over the name brands and their cost. I wanted to fit in, and the options available through parental choice didn't suit my personality at all. So, I began to buy the majority of my own clothing with my babysitting, dog-sitting, cat-sitting, newsletter-delivery, hard-earned dollars. You had a job? Aja'd do it. By the time I was in my early teens, I had set my sights on a certain aesthetic. It was 1995, and I was either wanting to dress like a hippie or a skater. Lucky for me there was one store in town that had both styles. Enter Harvest Trading Company.

Harvest Trading Company had two outposts, and it was a local business. It employed the very popular girls and sold exactly the clothing I wanted. It also sold candles, incense, mood rings, earring studs. It was a legitimate gateway to the Kingdom of Teendom. My first purchase was a skate tee (what's good, Stüssy?). There was nothing as coveted as the skate tee at the time, but I was later told by (sigh) a white boy that I was a "poseur" for wearing the shirt because I didn't skate. (Actually, I did, just not very well, and my board was big and clunky.) But either way, that was one of my earlier experiences with white gatekeeping of what I was "allowed" to like, but it certainly wouldn't be my last. At the time, that t-shirt cost me twenty dollars, which was roughly five to six hours of babysitting, depending on the client. In today's inflation that's $34.33. I was happy to pay for it and couldn't wait to count those hard-earned bills on the patchouli-scented counter of Harvest Trading Company. I knew what things cost, and I also knew the amount of work that went into being able to pay for them.

My next Harvest Trading Company purchase was a big-ticket item. The beloved item of the 1990s (and today): dungarees. I would have been delighted to get a pair from Osh Kosh B'Gosh but they were fifty dollars, which was no joke. Fifty dollars in 1995 is $85.82 in 2021. I didn't have that money, so I went back to my odd jobs. At the time Osh Kosh B'Gosh still produced their clothes in the US and still made adult sizes. When my birthday swung around, I was surprised with a pair of overalls from Harvest Trading Company, but they were not my beloved Osh Kosh B'Gosh. So, I asked if I could exchange them. I had to pay the extra twelve dollars for my Osh Kosh, but they felt so hard-fought and won. I wore them twice a week for two years until one of the legs ripped. That's hundreds of wears right there.

The point of the story is to remind you that, even as a teen-ager, I saved for the things I wanted. I recognize that just by being able to save, there is privilege there. Some teens take on part-time work to help their family out. I was fortunate to never be in that position. I didn't need five pairs of dungarees, just one good pair. I didn't have the options we have today, of course, but I never thought for a moment that Osh Kosh was charging too much for what was a premium product that provided good jobs for people. The price you pay often pays back.

THE BLACK FRIDAY TRICK

Now you know the rules of our society, so you know that in many ways our society runs off demonizing "others," including those in countries that are in or around the poverty line. We quietly demonize countries that have been traditionally pillaged or, in the case of Donald Trump, we loudly demonize them (see his "shithole countries" comment). In some ways we build the poor up with our pity (though some do this while dripping with quiet loathing), and in other ways we tear the poor down (probably born partly from our unacknowledged collective shame and ignorant thinking).

Those countries aren't economically poor because they've been pillaged again and again by more powerful countries who have robbed them of their resources for centuries; no, good sir, they're poor because of bad leadership and dictators (who have in no way been propped up by the more powerful countries who continue to rob and pillage; no, no, that never happens ever… how dare you even suggest it).

Those people aren't poor because capitalism is an unfair system that only rewards a few at the top while the majority at the bottom of the pyramid live in poverty. No, they're poor because they simply haven't worked hard enough in their lifetime (despite working-class jobs being some of the most challenging and back-breaking labor that keeps our society afloat).

There has always been this idea in our society that wealth distribution is a matter of sheer will, rather than luck and privilege.

As Lisa Adkins and Martijn Konings put it when writing for the *Guardian*: "There is no generational solidarity in the term 'millennials.' On the contrary, the fault lines that are now becoming highly visible—between millennials who stand to inherit assets and those who don't—have been produced by four decades of property inflation. Inheritance is becoming an increasingly important determinant of life chances."

On top of that, if we look at the numbers for the UK, buying property has changed dramatically since the 1990s. In 1995, buyers spent between 3.2 and 4 times their annual salary on property. In 2020, buyers spent on average ten times their salary. While wages have grown since the 1990s, the cost of property ownership has grown at a disproportionate rate. How can anyone afford to own any walls?

But tell me again about how all your wealth is determined through hard work and grit? Regardless, with all this information floating around about wealth distribution, it's still so shocking to me that others often act so callously to those without.

We see this every year in the lexicon we use to talk about Black Friday. Black Friday in recent years has become a heavily divisive holiday. When you see a news piece that shows Black Friday shoppers, scrambling and fighting over goods, it can quite frankly seem a little snotty. Look at those poor people fighting over material items! Consumerism is the worst! Except if you don't feel compelled to shop on Black Friday, that's probably because you have the privilege not to. Remember that. I mean, who really enjoys waking up at the crack of dawn to buy things that are supposed to be "affordable"? Not me. But some people participate in consumerism that way because that's how they can afford to buy needed essentials for their family, so it's important to demonize the system of consumption rather than the people who have less than you and shop only when it's affordable for them.

Black Friday is the name of the Friday which follows Thanksgiving (blech, ask me how I feel about that holiday on another day) in the United States. But the success of Black Friday soon spread outside of the US. The term "black" derives from accounting terms for finances. If your business is in the "red," you're in debt. If you're in the "black," that's where you want to be. Black Friday began in 1952, but it's becoming increasingly popular, with brands offering more and more outrageous deals to top the bargains of yesteryear. With Black Friday, sales frenzies have been growing more intense every year as folks have become more and more obsessed with the day, often camping outside of stores to collect their treasure upon the doors opening.

It's particularly revealing of the class divides and systems that this practice of lining up for goods that will improve your life has become something to be mocked. Especially to me, as I was one of many teenagers who camped out overnight with my friends to get concert tickets for popular shows destined to sell out, like the HFStival. Hell, lining up for concert tickets was a rite of passage. And even today no one mocks the hype baes who line up outside of Supreme stores for the latest drops of goods, which they might enjoy or choose to sell to another hype bae in another part of the world at an inflated price. Why? Because those are luxury goods with a very high resell value. (Though please, before you invest in the Supreme game, watch Hasan Minhaj's *Patriot Act* episode on the brand for some reference about what you're buying into. Although Supreme's owners recently sold the brand to VF Corporation, I think that episode still applies when questioning their popularity and what it was built off of. When Barbara Kruger herself feels inclined to refer to you as "a ridiculous clusterfuck of totally uncool jokers," it may be time to think about the ways in which you operate and who you steal from, or just question some of your life decisions.)

I remember my own experience shopping on Black Friday involved having to rise early with the sun, which is the energy my mother runs on, so I hated it, even if I was trying to get a discount on clothing I couldn't usually afford. By the time I was a teenager, I had decided I wasn't going to do it anymore because I had started to notice that often the stuff I really wanted wasn't marked down. Come to think of it, I never got a single good item from a sale either...just a lot of leftovers. Brands spent big money on the advertising of Black Friday leading up to the big day, going on and on about what amazing offers they have in store for you. And when the day came, I'd go into the store and the coat I wanted might have a small percentage off, but barely enough to make a dent in the actual price of the garment and not enough to make it affordable to me. The number of times I would mutter under my breath, "I got out of bed for a five percent discount?"

Instead, the big deals would be on merchandise you hadn't seen before and didn't especially want, but somehow felt compelled to buy because of the low, low, low cost. No, I didn't need this slightly shapeless blue turtleneck sweater (which I would hate by the following year), but it was really cheap and I'm here already...so I guess I'll buy it.

Coming home from Black Friday shopping always left me less than excited and somewhat unfulfilled, and I could never put my finger on why that was. Similar to the feeling after a fast fashion shopping spree, it felt like I had eaten a vast amount of low-fat chocolate. (I don't enjoy low-fat foods, ever. Full fat or bust.) Then, later in life, I learned about planned obsolescence and realized how much it factored into this hallowed day.

Planned obsolescence is a trick as old as time. Or as old as the automobile industry, to be exact. In Orsola de Castro's book *Loved Clothes Last*, she explains a brief history of planned obsolescence. It "started in the USA in the 1920s with General Motors, to encourage the buying of more cars, more often, and was originally intended as a way to increase production (and jobs) by deliberate manipulation of the design of a product, in order for it to break sooner."

Whiffs of planned obsolescence appear in other systems (especially electronics; Apple has had charges brought against it alleging planned obsolescence in their products), but in fashion it's a little different. It means making products that are far from superior in order to make a quick sale and have a customer who returns often to buy more goods (often to replace the goods they've just been sold). A friend of mine once told me that planned obsolescence was taught at the design school she attended. It's embedded in the fabric and texture of our culture. There's also a good argument here for how people within a certain poverty margin can't exactly stay ahead of the curve. If you always have to go for the twenty-dollar boots because that's all you can afford and they never last more than a season, next season you're buying another pair of twenty-dollar boots. I have good boots that I've spent about a hundred dollars on and which have lasted me years and years. All they need is resoling. I've had cheaper boots and found they're impossible to resole because the structure of the base simply doesn't allow for it, or they're made out of plastic, which a good-quality rubber sole wouldn't adhere to...deliberately. If you're not spending twenty dollars here and there just to get by, you can put that money into the next thing, which you will also invest in.

A good example of Black Friday planned obsolescence is when a popular electronics chain in the 1990s offered a DVD player for just twenty dollars. People lined up around the block for those DVD players at the crack of dawn. In the nineties, when I was a teenager, a good DVD player would set you back at least a hundred dollars new. Twenty dollars was unheard of. And, surprise, the "brand" that made the DVD player was unheard of, too. That's because cheaply manufactured goods that appear out of the blue are made *specifically* for events like Black Friday. These goods are assembled quickly with leftover bits. And, more often than not, they lack a warranty, fall apart quickly, and leave the customer out of pocket. Thus the loop continues and the consumption continues, because now you've got all the DVDs and nothing to play them on.

Even though I didn't register it in my teenage brain, I had begun to unconsciously register Black Friday as a scam in my head. The things that I really truly wanted were never on sale; it was just a ploy to get me in the store so I could spend money on things I didn't want or need but felt compelled to buy anyway in the frenzy of the moment. That's where that unfulfilled feeling came from.

And that's why Black Friday is a scam. A scam designed to get the most vulnerable trapped in a spending cycle.

THE FACTORY STORE TRICK

Later down the line I began to feel the same about "factory stores" and some "outlets" as I did about Black Friday. A long time ago I used to live for outlet shopping. From a young age I knew that clothing you loved never truly went out of style. I'm still the type of shopper who will fixate on something beautiful that I cannot afford for years, and search resell sites like eBay and Vestiaire Collective, until the piece pops up in my size. More often than not, it does. That tells you plenty about the amount of overproducing going on within the fashion industry. You can pretty much always find it secondhand if you're patient and wait long enough. My entire wardrobe is proof of that.

But I began to recognize in my youth that not all outlets are created the same. And today many are not. Where it used to be that outlets served as a place for last season's stock to go, in recent years the factory store has become king. Factory stores aren't outlets. They're stocked chock-a-block with low-grade goods that were produced to sell at lower cost made from cheaper materials.

Say you fall in love with a sweater from a brand you love, but it's out of your price range for what you're prepared to spend. Perhaps you'll visit the outlet and, lo and behold, they've got the sweater that you wanted! How could they possibly have it? It's current season (meaning it's currently in their stores full price)! That's because so often it's not the same sweater. The one being sold at the factory store is made of low-quality scratchy wool. The buttons are plastic, not the beautiful glass ones. It's like all the details that make one garment special are stripped from this other garment and replaced with materials of the lowest quality possible. But the changes aren't apparent to the untrained eye. Factory stores often aren't selling you anything you need or want; they're selling you a brand. You're better off buying a secondhand item online or from a charity shop that may have been worn gently but at least has some semblance of the quality you love and desire in a garment.

"CORPORATE SOCIAL RESPONSIBILITY"

"You mean that multinational brand lied to us?"...Well, perhaps they didn't lie to you, but they certainly massaged the truth, kneading their reality until we're convinced that actually, WE SHOULD SHOP BECAUSE THIS COMPANY IS DOING REALLY GOOD THINGS! Me buying this dress I don't need is actually *helping* someone!

And, yes, this multinational company probably did do a few of those things they bragged about on their corporate responsibility page, but this doesn't plaster over the fact that their name was mentioned in relation to that fire in Dhaka, Bangladesh, or that their cotton might have been picked by the Uighur people against their will.

Or that perhaps there's no way they can guarantee that all workers within their supply chain get paid properly.

Or that perhaps they don't treat their sales assistants that nicely.

So maybe they did actually do that crafting workshop with

fifty high-school students, who are also being absolutely bludgeoned with their advertisements day in and day out, telling them that if they don't buy a new outfit to be seen in on social media, they're not good enough.

Perhaps they did donate $100,000 to the World Health Organization during the COVID-19 pandemic, while simultaneously keeping all of their stores open in a time when health officials were telling us loudly that *everyone* (yes, sales associates and garment workers, too) should shelter in place. Sure, that donation is only 0.0007 percent of what the brand is valued at, but let's slap them on the back for it and praise their name (while their sales assistants message me because they're worried their colleague has COVID and is being forced to work and spread it around the store).

Cheers, lads.

Are you noticing a trend here? The pesky corporate responsibility pages end up being nothing but lip service when you look at the scale and scope of the problems in the various supply chains that are caused by these companies. Sure, you did a nice thing within your community in your neck of the woods. But what about the fact that the system that you profit from constantly oppresses people in traditionally pillaged countries? What are you actually doing to fix the root of the problem, rather than just a surface detail?

In fact, we have to start ignoring those corporate responsibility pages all together. I believe they're nothing more than a PR exercise for brands, and the esoteric language they use is to obscure real analysis of the facts. In a nutshell, they're there so you will continue to buy the clothes, but they challenge absolutely nothing of what's being said in these conversations.

We are so hardwired to shop and consume that we look for any reassurance that the companies we buy from are willing to do something about these bad systems; we want to overlook the lack of information presented to us. The disaster that had their products in among the rubble is *never* acknowledged on their website. No association. An inconvenient truth.

If a brand were being fair to their garment workers, garment workers would sing their praises. You know how if you're freelance and you have a client who's *really* on their game, you want to tell all your friends, "This is who you want to work for." Well, I've read a lot of interviews with garment workers while researching this book. And literally no one's saying that about anyone. But somehow we get weird assurance when a multinational corporation sticks a photo of a garment worker on their website under "corporate responsibility." Imagine how odd it would be if companies that employed us took our photos and slapped them on their website as proof that they do "good" stuff in the world. Look at us, feeding this freelancer in South London and keeping her lights on. Everyone praise us for paying her invoice on time! Maybe brands should simmer down with the stock photo images of East Asian women, because it feels pretty white savior-ish. Garment workers are your employees, too, who are an integral and necessary part of your business model (and let's not even go there with profitability), not someone you're doing a bit of charity work for. They're the reason your brand is worth billions. You paying them and treating them fairly is non-negotiable.

GREENWASHING

"But they're a sustainable brand!"

"How so?"

"Because they told me!"

"Did they now? What did they say?"

"They have a sustainable line."

"Oh, and what makes it sustainable?"

(Crickets chirping.)

Here's the thing, folks: a sustainable line *does not* make the brand or a corporation sustainable. That's nothing more than marketing. Sustainability cannot be a change in material; it must be a change in the entire way this system of exploitation operates. We call these brands' actions "greenwashing" (environmentalist Jay Westerveld coined the term in 1986, but the phenomenon actually dates back to the 1960s). Now the history of greenwashing comes from corporations, but one of the biggest culprits of it—where all great things like polyester fibers come from—is the fossil fuel industry!

According to Wikipedia, greenwashing is "a form of marketing spin in which green PR (green values) and green marketing are deceptively used to persuade the public that an organization's products, aims and policies are environmentally friendly." Did you know? "In the year 1969 alone, public utilities spent more than $300 million on advertising—more than eight times what they spent on the anti-pollution research they were touting in their ads," according to CorpWatch.org.

Greenwashing works in sneaky ways. For example, the Greenwash Fact Sheet published by CorpWatch in March 2001 states that "BP, the world's second largest oil company and one of the world's largest corporations, advertised its new identity as a leader in moving the world 'Beyond Petroleum.' It touted its $45 million purchase of the largest Solarex solar energy corporation. But BP will spend $5 billion over five years for oil exploration in Alaska alone." So solar panels, but drill, baby, drill...

And, what's more, greenwashing works, often churning out a profit for the culprits, especially if you have no idea how to identify it. So, naturally, the fashion industry has figured out ways to harness it. Almost every big brand has an *eco-friendly* line. Great. But if it accounts for less than 1 percent of the products listed for sale on their website that they're consistently churning out, then how does that line have *any* impact on preventing our climate emergency? *Well, it doesn't.* (And yes, I've gone through and counted the products before. The results are horrifying, but mostly I'm mad because they make me do math to get those low percentages.)

Unfortunately, when you visit many fashion websites that's exactly what you're presented with. Amazing fanfare and rolling out a plush green carpet for perceived sustainability efforts, but these overblown actions have very little impact.

What isn't sustainable and never will be:

- Having countless seasons a year (the times when you offer new clothes, which for many brands is *daily*).
- Offering endless amounts of stuff. At the time of writing, one popular fast fashion brand offers 13,333 styles of dress. Another one (which claims to be focusing on sustainability) offers 844 styles of dress. Another one, which is currently

ripping off a Black designer I know, just has an ominous 500+ dresses. Now this isn't total items for sale. This doesn't account for jackets, trousers, shoes, shirts, t-shirts, accessories, departments of other genders, and children. This is just dresses. A little choice is good. We all like choice. But this is too much. We're approaching planetary limits here with our resources. And it's almost like they don't want to acknowledge that. Or maybe they just want to pretend that we don't *know* that.

- Creating too much product at too cheap a price. Which means: if it doesn't sell, it can't even really be resold.

As the Union of Concerned Researchers in Fashion has put it: "This type of have-it-all environmentalism, achieved through market forces and satisfying growing consumer yearnings, is wholly incompatible with the reality of biophysical planetary limits."

> "What all of this means is that our planet is quickly running out of resources to make all this 'stuff,' and we're also running out of places to put it once its short life cycle is done."

What all of this means is that our planet is quickly running out of resources to make all this "stuff," and we're also running out of places to put it once its short life cycle is done. Most people who are truly committed to sustainability within the fashion industry know this, but many brands pretend they don't, and they expect us to be impressed by their recycled materials.

The amount of stuff being produced and turned over is a huge part of the problem, and no one wants to address that because it looks like smaller profit margins. But hey, quick, look over there at our recycling bins (which are mostly an incentive to get you in the store...*to buy more stuff*).

The truth is, while we all put our heads together to solve these problems, the burden should really rest mostly with the biggest corporations. The bigger your overall carbon footprint is, the bigger the responsibility you have on your shoulders to clean up *your* mess.

Here's some other fun greenwashing material gathered from corporate fast fashion websites.

- "[Our] headquarters in Los Angeles is the site of one of California's largest solar power installations."

Ooooh la la. How does one building with solar power installations in California positively affect someone in the Global South experiencing flooding currently?

- "Shipment boxes are recycled daily at our distribution center and in stores."

Chances are you and I recycle our boxes, too. Is anyone patting us on the back for that?

- "_____ is currently developing apparel collections using environmentally friendly materials."

What does that even mean? Technically, polyester is Earth-friendly, as fossil fuels do come from the Earth. This reminds me of the scientist in the film *Thank You for Smoking* who's been testing the link between nicotine and lung cancer for thirty years and hasn't found any evidence. "He could disprove gravity."

- "_____ provides 100 percent recyclable and reusable plastic and paper bags in many of its stores."

All paper and plastic bags can be reusable if you choose to reuse them. I can't believe someone got paid to write this drivel.

- "Awareness of and attention to the environmental and social impact of the fashion industry has rightly been increasing, and to reflect this we have been increasing our focus on responsible business activity."

All of this information has been widely available for years. *Years.* You've had decades to get your act together.

- "We have been working to develop a better understanding of our impacts, and a plan to improve our performance."

As above, why are you acting brand-new when this information has been available to you for *years?* What is not to understand about these issues, especially as you are at the literal center of them?

- "Modify: make changes to improve our environmental and social footprint."

What does this mean? What are you actually doing? What's the plan?

- "The pressures on our planet's limited natural resources and the challenge of climate change require prompt and concerted action from us all."

Why are you making me responsible when your owner is a billionaire? We don't all equally share the blame here, you know.

- "Boxes are used up to six times."

Woo me a little more with these fifteen pages of greenwash.

- "_____ will continue a strategy for fixture programs to be repurposed, and has also implemented an LED lighting strategy across stores to use up to 70 percent less electricity."

Great, I'll tell the garment worker who didn't get paid by you during the COVID-19 pandemic.

- "At _____, we work with brands such as X, Y, and Z who value sustainable practices in order to provide customers with options to make choices that will positively impact a cleaner future."

You work with hundreds of brands in your stores and websites, and probably thousands of suppliers. This is three. Why not give the consumer *all* sustainable brands? But you know what would be really cool? If your owner hadn't given donations to climate-denying politicians (looking at you, Rick Santorum). I know your owner doesn't like paying taxes. Dude even said that in an interview.

- "Normalize going into [our shops] for 'just socks' and coming out [with] three full shopping bags."

This tweet came from a popular chain that just launched a social media campaign called #____Cares. This campaign is supposed to focus on both the planet and its people. But you're either with sustainability or you're not. If we're all on the same page, and no one's offering "alternative facts," then you must recognize that consumption is a large part of the problem here. And yet in a single breath you're encouraging shoppers to normalize overconsuming from your shops. These brands know what they're doing.

I have visited countless fast fashion brands' websites, looking at those who turn over more than $20 million in profit a year, and not one of them acknowledges that the actual issue is their growth and scale and the fall-out pollution inflicted on the countries their products are made in. Their action toward mitigating problems is to claim that they're working with the suppliers, but from what we know in previous chapters...no one notified the suppliers of these facts.

Next time you visit the website of a bigger brand that you like, try to clinically separate the fact that you like their products from the language on the "corporate responsibility" page. Are they actually telling you anything at all? Check to see if your favorite brands' pages answer any of the following questions:

- Are they acknowledging any of the problems we've talked about in this book?
- Do they actively acknowledge the harm that the fast fashion cycle of consumption has done?
- Are they deprioritizing a growth-based economy?
- Do they focus on increasing the lifetime of garments?
- Do they talk about reducing the number of seasons they push on the consumer?
- Are they willing to work with the government to implement programs that recycle textile waste? (They can't check their own homework here...this needs to be regulated by an outside party!)
- Are they reducing their production? (Fewer clothes, better clothes.)

- Is there a garment worker on record that will vouch for this brand and the ways in which the job has positively impacted and enriched their life?
- Do they talk about the environmental impacts of their manufacturing in the countries they manufacture in? Not just about the preventive measures they claim to be taking, but the environmental harm already done and how they plan on mitigating it?
- Do they hold their hand up and say, "This is something we've done badly, and here's what we're going to do better to prevent this in the future"? As it's not enough to claim that you're cleaning up *your* mess if you're not mentioning what the mess actually looks like.

If you're not seeing any clear indication of these things, and a brand is profiting with millions and billions of dollars a year, this isn't a sustainable or an ethical brand. Sustainability plans have ultimately become marketing schemes. Because what we need most is...less.

And that doesn't help anyone's growth targets now, does it?

A brand's corporate responsibility is only as effective as the most marginalized member of their supply chain says it is.

WOKEWASHING

Black squares? What about them?

In June of 2020 the white world suddenly woke up to the movement of #BlackLivesMatter and realized how important and necessary it was. To many of us, this felt off. The idea that a movement can have existed for seven-odd years and been just as pressing and necessary during all that time, but suddenly white people decide to notice and take it seriously? Instead of movement toward deconstructing the racist systems our society is built upon, people on social media thought posting a black square as a show of solidarity was more effective. And then, of course, there was the necessary backlash because much of the black square posting came from brands and individuals who hadn't joined the racial justice conversation in a genuine way, often not even coming clean about the ways in which they had harmed Black people in the past.

What a mess.

One infamous case involved someone I consider a friend. Munroe Bergdorf is a transgender model and has broken so many barriers in just being her fierce gorgeous self, because you and I both know the world isn't safe for trans people or anyone outside of the rigid binary. I first heard about Munroe after she was released from a contract with a beauty brand for speaking about "white supremacy." Munroe is an outspoken advocate for transgender rights and fighting racism. The term "white supremacy" should never offend anyone. It's perfectly valid when we live in a world where white people are overrepresented in *most* positions of power. Often white people who aren't doing anti-racism work equate "white supremacy" with being called a "white supremacist." But the truth is you can still perpetuate quiet racism without riding around on horses at night wearing a white hood and burning crosses on people's lawns. Just like I can oppress transgender people because of my cisgender privilege by not consistently unpacking that privilege. You can harm someone without meaning to, and if you're unaware you'll often do exactly that, because you have your horse blinders on to the systemic injustices our society is founded on. And whether or not you meant to do harm doesn't outweigh the impact of that harm. So, there was Munroe Bergdorf minding her business, talking about the systems that oppress her and other people of color, and a lot of people got very offended about it, to the point where the general public pressured the beauty brand to release her from her contract. Three years later, the brand has since apologized to Munroe, and now the two work together in a friendly capacity. However, the brand was still *very* wrong in their initial actions, and it caused a lot of harm.

And here's where wokewashing comes into play. By initially signing Munroe Bergdorf, the brand received tons of social cachet for using a transgender mixed-race model in its campaigns. A lot of people sang the brand's praises for embracing groups of people largely left out of the conversation. But the brand should not have done this if it wasn't willing to listen to the very person it had leveraged for social capital when they explained societal oppressions that the brand did not understand. This isn't progressive; this is using an identity to wokewash the culture of your brand, when in actuality you yourself are *not* ready for those conversations.

Brands are ready to monetize anything, in a performative way, only when they don't think they will alienate any other stream of revenue. Big brands get social capital for featuring Black bodies while never doing the work to actually create meaningful change that makes it easier for Black people to exist in those bodies and in their spaces. After seeing what happened to Munroe Bergdorf I began to question if I could ever work with brands in any capacity if they were all too willing to toss us out like yesterday's trash for discussing race in a way that didn't center around white comfort. *Remember, reader, absolutely nothing changes if those with plenty of power feel completely comfortable with their station in life and all that power.*

FATPHOBIA

My work will always include bigger bodies, because the ways in which our society refuses to include bigger bodies is exclusionary and unjust. I don't even include fat bodies in the conversation around solving the massive fast fashion ecological problem, because the truth is plus-size people *do not have enough options* as it is, and don't have nearly enough clothing options to create an actual ecological crisis. You can see that when you visit a thrift shop and notice the limited number of items in plus sizes. When half the retailers won't make your size, your pickings are (ironically) slimmer than most.

The plus-size people I know have fewer options (in stores and elsewhere) and tend to wear their clothes a long time, in fear that the next time they need a new item they won't find anything available. Fast fashion has recently done a big show of including plus-size people, but sustainable fashion is painfully behind in this. So that is why every time a brand reaches out to me, I always ask them if size expansion is in their future plans (hey, other people with platforms...you should be doing *exactly* the same). If the answer is "no," our conversation ends there. That's really it. You want to dress only skinny people, why on Earth are you talking to me? Half these brands, I can't even fit into the clothes, which means they're viewing me as an asset but not seeing me as a full person.

A Note on Ethical Brands and Plus Size

When I finally found a designer who made beautiful ethical clothing (enter Lora Gene) and we launched a small capsule collection, it was because it was really annoying me that plus-size people weren't being considered by many sustainable and ethical brands, and the excuses, such as "I've heard that there is no market!" or "It's too expensive to produce!" sounded like fatphobia to me. To this day, that capsule collection remains one of the things I'm most proud of.

* Please do not message me and attempt to argue with me about whether or not plus-size inclusion should be necessary. If you don't like it, that's not my problem.

When we talk about colonialism and the patriarchy-enforced beauty standards, we don't chat enough about the ways in which these have lent themselves to perceptions of how our bodies "should" look. For example, the framework for BMI (body mass index) was created from mostly white, thin, European bodies. People come in all shapes and sizes, and what is one person's "healthy" is another person's "way too thin."

There's also this embedded notion in our society that you are meant to stay the same size throughout your life. And for some people that's how it goes (and there's certainly nothing wrong with that), but that's not the majority of bodies. And yet we treat bodies like that is the gospel and the truth. What about puberty? What about pregnancy? What about growing older? We truly have to ditch the idea that your body is going to stay exactly the same. It's not anything to aspire to. You don't get a medal for it.

But here's the thing: if we are building a "sustainable" landscape and we expect *everyone* to participate, we can't leave out plus-size people as the fashion industry traditionally has.

I became aware of the problem while I was still considered standard size. What that means is that most of the time I could walk into a store, move through the rack, and find something that might fit me. So throughout much of my twenties, I could wear many designers and brands... even though the world was still loudly screaming subliminal messages at me telling me I was fat—*funny that*. Trousers were the exception. Many designers will never ever design a pair of trousers that would fit me comfortably throughout the majority of my adult lifetime, because their designs don't account for curvier hips, thighs, and butts. And while I expected it, like I'd go to a sample sale of some designers and just skip the trouser section altogether, I still didn't think it was cool or fair. Now I think it's outrageous.

But more than that, BMI is now getting a fair amount of criticism, and fatphobia is being linked to racism. Dr. Sabrina Strings's work centers around some of this. For example, in her book *Fearing the Black Body*, she describes "how the thin bodies of northern and western Europeans were upheld as the ideal, while the often larger bodies of eastern and southern Europeans, as well as Africans, were considered signs of their inferiority. All of this was before we really knew anything about the (still blurry and confounding) relationship between weight and health. The modern BMI and its categories—underweight, normal, overweight and obese—have inherited much of that racism."

Ever watch a TV show or a film where the person's fat body is always the butt of the joke? Is that because it's funny? Is it? It isn't. Other things I hear about include tales of plus-size people having to buy two plane seats in order to fit comfortably. Plane seats are small because of corporate greed and wanting to fit as many people on the plane as possible for a low price. Business-class seats are usually bigger.

When someone with a bigger body goes to visit the doctor, it can be for any ailment, but every plus-size person knows that, depending on the doctor, they might well be asked the million-dollar question:

"Hi, I think I broke my arm."

"Shame, but have you thought about losing weight?"

"What's that got to do with it?"

I've been on either side of the metaphorical scale and, I can tell you, the world is a whole lot nicer to you when you're smaller. But when I was "standard size," it never dawned on me that a plus-size person can't walk into any shop and buy clothes straight off the rack like I could. That's what thin privilege is: it's not noticing how challenging it is for anyone who isn't thin. Even before I myself was plus size, I began to realize that as a standard-size person I needed to advocate for plus-size bodies! Because I listened to my friends, and that's checking your privilege, right? Now that I am a plus-size person, I'm really careful to not take up too much metaphorical room in the conversation. Fat-body acceptance hasn't been something I've had to work through my entire life, so it wouldn't make sense for me to be the loudest voice in the room, constantly holding the mic. But one thing I can do is push *all* brands who want to work with me to make clothing that includes everyone. When I first began this act, I was immediately put off by all the excuses brands gave. Now of course I get that smaller brands can only make a few sizes to begin with, especially if your clothing isn't made to order. But many of the excuses I heard just sounded like: "No, because we don't want to."

Fine.

But don't make it seem like it's rocket science to scale up a pattern, because I see a lot of small brands doing it every day in an effort to be more inclusive. I have gotten so sick of the ways in which our society makes excuses for not including larger bodies. If we want a more sustainable future, that looks like dressing all bodies, no ifs, ands, or buts.

Much of the world treats fat bodies like they do not deserve to show up happily, beautifully, and well dressed. And that stops with me. Fight for everyone to dress themselves while we're tackling the other problems. Let it end with us.

SUPPLY, INTEREST, DESIRE, DEMAND, REPEAT

The nature of the world we live in and our relationship to products is volatile and ever-changing; something priceless can become underpriced, something valueless can become valuable.

Our value system is based on supply, interest, desire, and demand.

- Something that is not in "**supply**" often becomes **desired**, of **interest**, and in **demand**.
- Something that isn't in "**demand**" is ultimately valueless, even if it was once in high demand.

- Something that isn't **"desired"** has shorter shelf life and quickly loses value.
- Something that isn't receiving **"interest"** often has to be removed or destroyed due to the cost of warehousing.

If we view these quantifiers in our discussion about fast fashion, we start to understand why this model should never have a place in our value system. The clothing loses its value far too quickly, both in the consumer's mind and in the general market, because there's too much of it and it isn't very good. It saturates both the market and the general clothing landscape, and this means its already low value decreases ever further. Which in turn means there is very little room for reselling, because the value of the clothing had already decreased upon purchase, and the quality can never hold up on resale. Fast fashion is similar to a new car, in the sense that it massively decreases in value the moment you take it off the lot.

The fact that fast fashion will never be able to participate in an enlightened value system is the reason stores have to clear out stock from their inventory to make room for new merchandise. It's also why we hear about clothing being destroyed. Brands do that both because there is too much but also in order to maintain the "integrity" of the brand and create artificial demand. And if discount stores didn't exist, we'd have a whole lot more waste in the world, because the scale of our production means that there's frequent "clearing out," also called "seasons."

It's got to stop. It's all got to stop. And I think we can help make it happen.

PART TWO

8

LET'S GET COMMITTED

Are you one of the many people who has never written a letter to an elected official or a brand before in your life? Are you feeling guilty right now because of that sentence and your lack of action?

Listen up, this is a guilt-free book, so put that guilt away. It does nothing for anyone, least of all those you feel guilty about. Instead, let's do something with it.

Don't sweat it: a lot of people don't know where to begin with this stuff. It all feels too overwhelming. We feel like our voices aren't useful and don't have the power to create change because we have been told to feel this way by the bad system that governs us. They are the ones who make us feel small.

But, listen up and listen carefully.

YOU ARE SO POWERFUL.

EVERY DECISION YOU MAKE ON THIS PLANET HAS AN EFFECT.

So it's time to build up your toolkit with tools that are going to come in handy when we start the "learning" section of this book.

Think of this like a way better version of an IKEA flatpack kit. It will get technical occasionally, and you'll have to examine things a few times before you can identify how they fit properly; a couple of errors in judgment and reassessments will be inevitable. But I'm here to explain stuff, rather than just asking you to follow some frustrating diagram with lots of numbers (my dad is the King of Putting Together IKEA Furniture Wrong...but he always gets it in the end, with a brick or an extra bolt or two). No one said it would be easy, but the good news is you will have learned a lot in the process, and there's no perfect way to do activism other than trial and error!

So, I need you to make a promise to yourself right now, that once we have worked through all of this, you're not going to be silent about the broken systems anymore. Use that voice you have. (If you don't do it for any reason other than spite, still...go for it.)

I'M A FAN OF AN OLD-FASHIONED LETTER

I know some people prefer emails, but we spend enough time looking at screens, and emails are rather easy to delete and avoid. And the truth is, letters sometimes have more of an impact than people realize, especially when *a lot* of letters arrive in a mailroom about one topic. Plus...it's a lost artform (go, US Postal Service and Royal Mail).

Did you know that many corporations and brands have a policy that if they receive a certain number of comments about one particular topic, it has to get addressed in meetings and boardrooms?

Now, whether or not they choose to actually do something is a completely different story. But if you speak up for any reason at all, do it to be a thorn in someone's side. Do it for the planet, which is getting consistently trashed by this process. Do it for the garment worker who's working hard enough. Do it because a lot of us talking about the same thing can't be ignored (that's how you get something trending, after all). Not everyone has the capacity to get in the streets, and the notion that everyone can and should is rooted in ableism. Not everyone has the same amount of free time. But if you have a spare ten minutes and you've got a pen and a paper, perhaps take a moment and jot down some thoughts.

I'm a pretty seasoned letter writer, so I'm going to give you a template here for addressing both politicians and big box stores.

Dear [insert Elected Official's name here],

Recently I learned about the scale of the problems in the fashion industry. It really horrifies me that the climate emergency that our planet is quickly speeding toward is aided by consumption of fashion garments. It bothers me that brands often owned by billionaires pay their garment workers pennies, while they themselves make a fortune. Overproduction within brands plays a part in all of this, and it must be stopped. Additionally, consumers and citizens are left with the problem of dealing with the cleanup process when in actuality the companies themselves should be responsible, not the taxpayer (or the citizens of countries overseas). I was wondering if you yourself have considered how these industries are harming the planet. As a citizen I'm very concerned, and that's why I'm writing to you today. I was wondering if you have considered a few things that we could do.

The fashion industry needs to reduce carbon consumption to 1990 levels in order to tackle some of the environmental hazards we face.

We need to push corporations for *full* transparency within their supply chain in order to ensure that all workers are paid a fair and living wage.

Synthetic fibers are responsible for microplastics within our water supply. We should be looking into the idea of reducing the amount of new synthetic fibers produced every year.

For citizens, many of these solutions require action from leaders like yourself. Like for instance, currently, textile recycling is hard on people, and we recycle on average only 1 percent of textiles. We need to recycle more and create more from recycled garments. But first we need systems in our society to recycle more of our old clothing easily. We could build these systems, but companies over a certain size should be taxed more in order to pay for these systems. You've got to clean up the mess.

I look forward to hearing how and when you are going to start.

HOW TO PLAY SOCIAL MEDIA

If you really aren't into writing letters (and have tried; really do, it is so fulfilling) then you can take your issue to the wider public through social media. Whether you have a micro (between 1,000 to 100,000 followers) or macro (influencer with more than 150,000 followers) profile, you will hold an audience, and a percentage of that will be people who you can influence, aka they will listen and digest your thoughts. Cause and effect.

I'm not exactly sure of the optics here, because the big social media companies aren't exactly transparent with their algorithms, but I know from a few hashtags in my past that all it takes is a handful of bigger Twitter accounts using the same hashtag to get it moving along and trending. I've had two hashtags that trended on Twitter.

The first one was #AmericaInFiveWords. I created this hashtag around the time that twelve-year-old Tamir Rice was brutally murdered at the hands of the law in 2014. At the time, I was living in Virginia with my parents, and I felt like I lived in two Americas. Black people I knew were literally scared to do things like jog alone or drive at night. I once participated in a thread where Black people who enjoyed running talked about no longer running at night and no longer running while wearing hoodies. This was long before the tragic death of Ahmaud Arbery in 2019, who was pursued and fatally shot while jogging unarmed in Georgia. I was starting to feel quite claustrophobic in America, but even more shocking to me was that it felt like the white people I knew had no clue. They simply had no idea that, while they blithely discussed feeling like their rights were being stripped because the controversial film *The Interview* wasn't being distributed, their Black neighbors and friends were having discussions about the long list of things that were frankly dangerous for Black bodies. I was so angry, and I couldn't believe it was invisible to them. I wanted to start a conversation that illustrated that there were two Americas and that, depending on the color of your skin, you might view America one way or another. So I asked two big Twitter accounts how they would sum up #AmericaInFiveWords. And that was really all it took. It took off like wildfire, spreading all over the internet. Once it went, it couldn't be contained, and by the end of the weekend there were hundreds of thousands of tweets (many from white people who were screaming hateful racist things at me, which is, of course, tons of fun...I even got one death threat). The tweets associated with the hashtag were by turns funny and striking, like "you want fries with that?" or "justice is not equally applied." But it was illuminating. It did exactly what it was supposed to do: it highlighted how differently America was viewed by different people, often those differences hinging on your level of safety. It showcased to the wider world how splintered the country was.

The second hashtag I've made that became popular was #IQuitFastFashionBecause, which I started in 2020. The thought process behind that more recent hashtag was to drown out some of the noise happening on Black Friday, with fast fashion and the conspicuous consumption being pushed in every which direction, and get people to realize that these purchases absolutely have weight. We may pay a low price, but someone else elsewhere is paying a pretty steep price for that garment we didn't really need. So many of our online purchases happen quickly, without a lot of thought behind hitting the purchase button. I wanted to put some tweets in everyone's timeline that highlighted the effects that all these purchases had on the world, so that maybe the person who felt compelled to shop, and didn't even know why, would pause for a minute and question that.

WAYS TO LEARN ACTIVELY

If we're getting really deep into specific actions within the fashion industry, I've got a few ideas where to start. If we're talking about solving wage inequality, both domestically and abroad, we need to support workers. Support the "Fight for $15" minimum wage movement in the US. When everyone gets paid a fair wage, that makes a more even playing field for everyone.

If we're talking about the United Kingdom, the Environmental Audit Committee's 2019 report "Fixing Fashion: Clothing, Consumption and Sustainability" is a great place to start and really sink your teeth in. The report is long, so brace yourself and don't overwhelm yourself by attempting to read it all at once. But what's really great is to focus on the recommendations that were given to members of Parliament. There are all sorts of suggestions that put the onus on the industry and corporations (right where it should be), while allowing space for government bodies to regulate. These recommendations would help slow the pace, treat others fairly, and lessen the environmental burden of the industry. But I am going to break it down for you.

- The "Fixing Fashion" report calls for transparency within the supply chains and for strengthening of the Modern Slavery Act.
- It advocates for research "to be carried out urgently into the occupational health risks of working with synthetic fibers." Something we all need. I mean, in 2020 microplastics were found in a baby's placenta. Grim.
- It suggests funding for an "end of life" cycle for clothes. "A charge of one penny per garment on producers could raise £35 million for investment in better clothing collection and sorting in the UK. This could create new green jobs in the sorting sector, particularly in areas where textile recycling is already a specialist industry such as Huddersfield, Batley, Dewsbury, and Wakefield in West Yorkshire."

• Finally, it suggests that **"Retailers must take responsibility for the social and environmental cost of clothes."** Couldn't agree more.

Read through all the suggestions provided, find a few that really resonate with you, and write to your local political representative to put it on their radar, too. The more people speak up about these pressing matters, the more momentum the movement gains. The conversation needs your voice!

Someone who has been speaking up since 2012 is Elizabeth Cline, the New York–based expert on fast fashion, labor rights, and sustainability in the apparel industry. She notes: "To name a few examples of innovative laws, in California the Garment Worker Protection Act aims to raise wages for garment workers to the minimum wage, and more importantly holds brands accountable when wage theft and poverty pay emerge in factories. Currently, brands aren't liable for what happens in factories, and we've seen where that lack of accountability can take us. Similarly, in Europe, we're seeing the introduction of much stronger human rights due diligence laws like the German Supply Chain Law (still in the draft phase), which would require that companies prevent and remedy human rights and environmental violations in their supply chains; companies would also be sanctioned or fined for violations, giving the law teeth. We are expected to see similar legislation in the US as well." She adds: "I would argue that throwing your support behind a global minimum tax is also a good thing to consider. The global minimum tax is something being proposed in the US by Secretary of the Treasury Janet L. Yellen. The aim of the tax is to help end the race to the bottom. It will ultimately de-incentivize the idea that you can take all your business overseas for cheaper labor. Yes, the cheaper labor will of course be there, but...you will pay a price for seeking it out in that way. I say yes to this. We could help raise the standards for domestic production as well."

If you're overwhelmed at the idea of getting started, Elizabeth points out: "One of the biggest myths about systemic reform is that it happens from the top down, from those in power just deciding things need to change. But real change happens from the grassroots up via groups of dogged, committed citizens dedicated to a cause. You don't need to be an expert or even have experience in organizing. You have a right as a citizen and as a human to fight for what you believe in. I recommend getting involved with an existing protest movement, political party, nonprofit organization, or campaign that's advocating for change. Fashion is connected to everything: race, class, gender, environment, land, waste, animal rights, agriculture, colonialism, culture, and so on. There's a lot of work to be done, so do a little work to find a group working on something you're very passionate about, and volunteer to see if it's a good fit."

So, there you have it, step up and join in:

- Write a letter.
- Send an email.
- Start a hashtag that holds an inequality to account.

Use your voice. It will always be heard.

9

LET'S TALK ABOUT US

The next step in the uncomfortable unpacking of all your consumer baggage requires you to understand your place on the consumer scale, and why you hold it, because when we talk about consumption it's important to recognize who is consuming at the expense of the entire planet...and who is not.

Part of the mind-frame around consumption must be looked at through the same lens as the one we look through when we inspect global wealth: who holds it and who doesn't. The lens we use to look at wealth can also be used to scrutinize power.

According to an Oxfam media briefing on "Extreme Carbon Inequality" on December 2, 2015, "The poorest half of the global population—around 3.5 billion people—are responsible for only around 10 percent of total global emissions attributed to individual consumption, yet live overwhelmingly in the countries most vulnerable to climate change...while the richest 10 percent of people in the world are responsible for around 50 percent of global emissions." So what does that mean? It means the calls are coming from inside the house. Most likely, my house and your house, too, if you're reading this book. You probably don't consider yourself a wealthy person if you're reading this. That's because we live in a society where people actively sidestep the conversation about privilege, wealth, and global resources. This creates a situation in which no one wants to bear the actual responsibility of reconciling themselves with societal and environmental problems that they have caused, and that still continue to be made by (predominantly privileged) humans.

But before we even dive into this conversation on consumption, first I need to make it clear that...can I just say...a hundred companies are responsible for 71 percent of all carbon emissions.

Read that again: a hundred companies are responsible for 71 percent of all carbon emissions. Surprise! This is actually a pretty well documented fact that was first reported in the "CDP Carbon Majors Report 2017," which was published in collaboration with the Climate Accountability Institute. But the reason that these companies are responsible for this percentage of carbon emissions is that those fossil fuels are being used for our consumption, yours and mine. The sooner we move away from fossil fuels as a planet, the better for everyone (except for the people who have made billions of dollars off fossil fuels). But how far does the fossil fuel industry reach, and what does it have to do with your wardrobe?

Well, let's start with the fabric. In 2016, the entire world began to pay attention to Indigenous environmental injustice surrounding Standing Rock and the Dakota Access Pipeline. The pipeline was an initiative proposed by Energy Transfer Partners. The oil pipe itself was originally supposed to run close to the state capital of Bismarck but was rerouted after it was deemed "too risky" for Bismarck's water supplies! Another horrendous act of crime against Indigenous people, from a very long list in the United States. But how many who participated in the demonstrations, whether in person or online, recognized in that moment that the oil that runs through those pipelines also feeds our insatiable taste for fast fashion? Because, guess what, synthetic fabrics such as polyester, nylon, Lycra, synthetic fur, and acrylic (which is in so many places you'd never expect it to be, like most yarns, as it helps to bond fibers together) all come from…fossil fuels.

According to the Ellen MacArthur Foundation in their 2017 report "A New Textiles Economy: Redesigning Fashion's Future," 98 million tons of non-renewable resources, "including oil to produce synthetic fibers, fertilizers to grow cotton, and chemicals to produce, dye, and finish fibers and textiles," were used for the textile and garment industry. These are things that many clearly do not consider when we talk about the fossil fuel industry. So when we talk about the fossil fuel industry, we need to look at *every* industry that utilizes and draws on this bastion of power. The industry is so insidious, and has roots in so many aspects of our lives. And that includes our wardrobes.

But why do we have closets full of clothes, and why do we keep on buying more? Let's talk about you. Me. Us. Because this will help us to understand exactly where we fall in all of (looks around at the burning trash fire that is all our systems of consumption and waves hands)…this.

ARE YOU REALLY POOR OR DO YOU JUST FEEL POOR BECAUSE OF CONSPICUOUS CONSUMPTION?

I grew up in a very affluent area in a working-class family. The definition of what qualifies as "working class" definitely changes, depending on whom you ask, but I would argue that my family is working class. Because I'm American, let's use the American standard of working class, which can also include low-level white-collar workers, to which group my father belongs, and my mother, who was a schoolteacher, was definitely working class. There was no safety net for my parents if things didn't go according to plan, and their work was their only form of security. We had the privilege of upward mobility, which is not afforded to every Black family in America...but there's a huge difference between privilege that comes from sacrifice and privilege that comes from generational wealth. Of which my family has none. I was discussing this exact topic with my friend who is an inclusion consultant, Rabya Lomas. We were chatting about our childhoods and the similarities, as I am Black and Rabya is Pakistani. We both recognize how privileged we are today, but we also had parents who had zero safety net in our upbringing. Describing her upbringing and her parents, Rabya says, "Not poor but not exactly rolling in it either. Able to get on the property ladder eventually, afford a mortgage and send three kids to university, but at the expense of not having much left over. Still having to work today, even though they really ought to be retired."

Both my parents still work, too, and the similarities in our experience isn't missed by me. Both Rabya and I spend a lot of time talking about wanting to give back to our parents for the sacrifices they made for us to have better. "I think that's the difference to those with generational wealth. Fundamentally, there is no sacrificial element. Both generations are able to live in financial ease. No one goes without," says Rabya.

I was fortunate that my parents did well for themselves. They were both college-educated, as they had access to student loans. (I remember the year my mother finally paid off her student loans, and the look of relief on her face and the joy she felt. I didn't quite understand what the debt meant, but I completely understood her sense of relief.)

Anyway, I grew up in a very affluent area, where test scores were high and taking grade-level math in high school was something I hid from my peers (as many of them were taking math courses above their grade level). The idea of going to vocational school instead of university, senior year, was frowned upon...of course in a silent and very insidious way. Our high school had a wall where all the graduates put their names up, along with the school they would be attending, on a cut-out profile of a graduation head and bust. I remember only seeing one vocational school. There's absolutely zero wrong with vocational school. Our society wouldn't function without people doing all sorts of jobs (plumbers, mechanics, carpenters), but vocational school signified something shameful about your socioeconomic status that went unspoken yet held us all in its system. This is how power and opportunity inequality work; they are silent governors of us all, but they are never openly spoken about. It's why, contrary to popular belief, we will never get ourselves out of the mess which is systemic racism if we just all "stop talking about race so much," because numerous reports and statistics show that there is inequality present in all aspects of life, from home ownership to health outcomes. The route out isn't quick and it isn't clear, and it holds us all in the place in which we were born. These methods of silence have been used to perpetuate some of the worst oppression in our society. If you don't have the vocabulary to talk about the harmful system that clearly exists, then those who benefit from the harmful system can claim that the system doesn't actually exist at all. And this starts when you are young, and it's why vocational school was stigmatized and university was revered. It's why people like me feel ashamed about taking a grade-level math class...and so the gap widens. This is the system which has been created so that shame is allowed to fester and inhibit growth.

Growing up in an affluent area can really mess with one's perception of self. For the vast majority of my life I considered my own family "poor." We weren't. I was just surrounded by people who were far richer than we were. Let's look at some of the ways Resource Generation qualifies "poor and working-poor," and you can decide whether it's fitting for you as well:

- *"Substandard, unstable, or inconsistent housing"*

Nope. We always had a roof over our head and never worried about that.

- *"Underemployed/underpaid, sometimes long-term use of public benefits"*

My family has never been on benefits.

- *"Little access to higher education"*

My parents made sure we all went to university, even if they had to sacrifice.

- *"Chronic lack of health care, food, or other necessities"*

We always had health insurance through my dad's job. I asked my dad if staying at his job for forty-one years was a sacrifice on his part, and he responded, "Not exactly. Many of us in general (BIPOC people, sometimes white women as well) stay at our jobs because we feel like it's a risk to move to another job and leave a secure job for uncertainty. Once you got security at a job, you stayed there. Now why is it a risk? Because of racism and sexism. We haven't come to where we need to be to allow people to be hired on the content of their character."

- *"Frequent involuntary moves, chaos, and disruption of life"*

My parents live in the house which they moved into when I was one.

- *"Often raised with strong value on resource sharing and taking care of each other"*

Okay, I feel like this is many BIPOC individuals and family I know. This one fits.

- *"Targeted and incarcerated disproportionately by the state generally and specifically through systems like child protective services, vagrancy laws, immigration enforcement, and money/cash bail"*

As a child I was notoriously clumsy, always tripping and falling (I had hearing damage in one ear, which aids to it). And so one time my mother took me to the doctor for a regular checkup, and she felt uncomfortable with the line of questioning being pointed at her by the doctors. In a nutshell, they were itching to call child protective services because of my self-inflicted bruises and scrapes. That's racial profiling for you.

- *"Intellectual, artistic, and labor contributions frequently stolen, co-opted, or made invisible in dominant society"*

Ooof, talk about cultural appropriation.

Okay, so most of those qualifiers really did *not* fit me. At all. A few, but let's get real. We weren't poor.

Also note that, according to Resource Generation, the "poor and working-poor," who make up "approximately 20 percent of the population, control roughly 1 percent of US total net worth." Well, those are certainly not the people keeping these companies in billion-dollar profits.

Growing up, I knew there was a wealth divide, which was of course also made worse by the fact that I stuck out like a sore thumb because of my Blackness in what was a predominantly white elementary school during my years in attendance.

I wasn't poor, but I was made to feel poor because I never had the "right" clothes growing up, and much of what I wore included hand-me-downs and thrifted options; I was surrounded by snobs. I remember a kid asking me in the third grade if I wore the same clothing every day. I did not. But barbed insults like that stick with you and inform and coercively control your mindset as an adult, especially when it comes to consumption habits. I remember clearly hating the sweater my mother convinced me to wear in my fourth grade school photo. It was a pastel yellow and blue V-neck from the brand Ocean Pacific. The worst thing about wearing hand-me-downs was the age gap between me and my older sister (five years). We were children of the eighties and teens of the nineties. And if you look at the sartorial styles of those decades, they changed rapidly during that time period. A sweater that my sister wore in 1987 looked dated and very out of place in 1992. When I got to school that day, I was teased without mercy. We try and pretend these things don't sting and stick with us, but they completely inform who we become as adults. I never felt enough because of my upbringing.

I wasn't poor, but I was made to feel poor because my parents lived in a townhouse (a terraced house in a beautiful neighborhood), while many of my elementary school classmates lived in big, newer, detached single-family homes.

I wasn't poor, but I was made to feel poor because I always had part-time jobs at a young age for my spending money. That was just our parents' way of teaching us the value of money: we had to earn it ourselves and were never given an allowance. So I would spend weekends dog sitting, babysitting, and doing a host of other odd jobs, when many of my other classmates spent their weekends at sleepovers.

I wasn't poor, but I was able to buy my own clothes from age eleven. I was lucky to have the agency to do so, because my mother and I didn't see eye to eye on what I wanted or needed... but I still felt very poor.

I wasn't poor, but I was made to feel poor because my parents could never help me buy a house in northern Virginia in my twenties, while so many of my peers had help from generational wealth.

I wasn't poor, but I was made to feel poor because my dad brought me to TV sets as a teenager, and I soon found myself working every summer on them as a production assistant and camera assistant, instead of sitting at the pool with my peers. My dad knew that getting us in the door was important for our future survival. It just so happened that those TV jobs enabled us to travel outside of the country, which infinitely broadened my horizons and is arguably the reason I'm sitting here typing to you from my dining-room table in London.

All these things made me feel very poor at the time.

In fact, all these things actually made me normal. The vast majority of the world doesn't have generational wealth in that way. But they still made me feel "poor" at various times in my life. Yet it's actually ridiculous looking back at it, because we always had enough to eat and presents under the Christmas tree. There was never a stress of how an electricity bill would be paid or whether we would be evicted from our house. My mother loves a coupon and has always budgeted, but it didn't equal poverty despite her often telling us we "didn't have a pot to pee in." (The origin of that phrase comes from the Great Depression. Families that were really hard up would collect their urine in a big pot for the leather tanneries to use in exchange for a small fee. If you didn't have a pot to pee in, you were really in a bad place.)

There's a massive difference between "feeling poor" and "being poor," but so often many of us who are nowhere near the poverty line conflate those feelings with actual poverty. Poverty is a system of oppression that's very hard to escape from. From a young age I had internalized a supposed lack of "abundance" with being poor. But all of this is due to growing up in an area where there was probably an unhealthy amount of abundance and excess. Society can be divisive, and these feelings are pernicious. When you live in a townhouse but your area is surrounded by McMansions, it's an easy mistake to fall prey to.

My mother grew up without much in a family of nine Black kids in Jim Crow–era Alabama, so the fears of poverty have always followed her throughout her life. It's a hard thing to shake, and in some way that mindset permeated our household, too. As well as all the frugal habits. We didn't waste a thing in my family.

So, with all these feelings swimming around, I felt "poor" and I felt lacking. Which is why I was already naturally indoctrinated into becoming the perfect consumer of fast fashion! I was someone who had enough disposable income, and who never felt "good enough" in relation to my peers. I looked at what was on offer and thought "This is for me! Finally, I can dress like everyone else, in a way of keeping up appearances with new clothes, whenever I want!"

This is what I would say really started me on the path of fast fashion consumption, and I believe that it's the same for millions and millions of us. It fills the gaps that our society makes us feel we have in ourselves and our lives. The void that never fitting in left in me. Perhaps this could be plugged by buying myself a place in the world and concealing these insecurities in piles of clothing?

It is important for you to understand your own sense of lacking, and whatever engendered it at this stage in your journey, because it will explain what drives this sense of not being enough that forces you to acquire more.

LISTEN UP, THE INSECURITIES YOU HAVE BEEN GIVEN ARE NOT YOURS

We all have wounds dating back to childhood that affect how we interact with systems of injustice, some deeply embedded and others less so, depending on our place in the hierarchy. Class and race are the two things I think about most. Respectability politics in the Black community play a huge part in how you're dressed and looking "presentable." This is the aftermath of colonialism! All of it shows up where you least expect it. When you're an ethnic minority, you're always quietly striving for an unattainable level of perfection in order to be a "model minority" in a system that both sees you enough to "other" you and completely ignores you when you don't serve a purpose.

I'm of the generation that thinks anyone could benefit from therapy (but access to therapy, and the lack thereof in our society, is a completely different book, which someone much more knowledgeable than me has written or is writing). I ended up struggling so hard to undo so many negative habits linked to classism, racism, and childhood harassment over my wardrobe and lack of "cool" clothes. So much so that, even a few years ago, I still couldn't bear to wear the same thing two days in a row. That barb really stuck around in my psyche for years. This, coupled with my first interaction with racism, when a kindergarten classmate told me, "Black people smell," and it's a real recipe for complexes you didn't even realize you were battling. To this day I am still terrified of smelling bad. When you grow up an ethnic minority (or a poor white person) in an affluent white area, you just want to blend in, and if you're ostracized for your clothes or the way you look, compounded with the feeling of being an outsider already...it builds something terrible inside you. You internalize this otherness and it sits deep inside you ready to be manipulated.

It dawned on me that the comments I received in my formative years still had control over the decisions I made as an adult.

So, a few summers ago, I challenged myself to wear a dress that I loved two days in a row. It became neither smelly nor stained. It was a revelation. Those comments could no longer hurt or control me. The truth is that we put a lot of emphasis on how the outside world views us, and often that emphasis is exaggerated because of our insecurities.

But these very insecurities are what the marketers and advertisers prey on and invest in. The currency of insecurity is strong in the market and open to attack and exposed to manipulation. The big brands know we buy when we have an occasion we want to prove ourselves in, be that a job interview or a date, because once upon a time we were told we weren't worthy of that job or that person's interest. Or that we couldn't wear a dress two days in a row. They tell you to have a new outfit for a Christmas party so your boss might see for the first time that you are worthy of promotion, or to buy some new swimwear so people judge you less on a beach. Or that you need a Birkin bag to be taken seriously because you're a Black girl entering the "professional world." They do this because *they know you*. They track you. They watch your purchasing. When you are more likely or less likely to buy. When you feel insecure. Their cookies track you and push stuff onto you when you need help the most because the world has been assaultive to you. Buy this and you can be this.

All of this explains the speed at which fast fashion turns over, and how it is marketed to us. On any given day, I might be served hundreds of advertisements in subtle ways. Teeth whitening. Clothing. More clothing. More clothing. Dating sites. Fast food. TV shows. If I were a billionaire I'd launch a campaign of targeted ads that just said, "You're good enough as you are," rather than launch a car into space. It'd serve our society better for sure. The advertisements I see might as well say: "YOU'RE RIGHT (and those kids at school were right, too): YOU'LL NEVER BE GOOD ENOUGH AS YOU ARE. WE SEE YOU, BUT WE CAN HELP YOU BE BETTER IF YOU BUY FROM US."

And don't get me started on social media. If fast fashion grew rapidly in the last twenty years (and it did), guess what else was growing at the same time? Social media. Social media, particularly Instagram, has almost certainly played an unprecedented part in your ideas of what an acceptable *you* should look like. And with the recent closure of so many brick-and-mortar stores—which has only accelerated as a result of the COVID-19 pandemic—a report by McKinsey & Company in December 2020 predicted that "brands will engage even more closely with social media to offer shoppers exclusive content and personalized experiences." You think you're served ads now? We're only just getting started. And, unfortunately, this has a real solid effect on the youth of today, and it's not good.

The *New York Times* did a piece in 2019 entitled "What Do Gen Z Shoppers Want? A Cute, Cheap Outfit That Looks Great on Instagram" in which they interviewed several teenagers about their shopping habits. The takeaway for me was that teenagers really don't want to be seen wearing the same item of clothing twice on Instagram. You see the problem there? Our world has created a society with messaging that wearing the same thing twice isn't cool. And we have to reverse that, because it's a huge part of the problem. If we don't reverse it, we are essentially confirming our internalized insecurities and letting them control who we are and how we feel about the bodies we live in.

10

WE NEED COLLECTIVE CHANGE

If you asked me where the problems were in this entire fast fashion system, I'd have one answer for you: multinational corporations.

Especially ones that have billionaires at the top, when we're all very much aware that the garment workers who make the clothes don't even get a percent.

Who does this system benefit on a grand scale?

The planet?

The people?

Or a select handful of very wealthy people, while the rest of us are left with a closet full of clothes we felt compelled to buy for reasons we can't explain and no longer even like?

Next stop, the landfill.

Or Ghana.

Who does this system benefit?

How has this system of hyper-consumption made our world better?

Ask yourself these questions once more.

Who does it serve? And whose life does it better?

Obviously not every multinational corporation is up to bad things all the time, but the entire system of colonialism is the operating brain behind our current flawed system. The idea that you can have a corporation in one country that manufactures halfway across the world because this improves its profit margins, but does not help raise the vast majority of folks who work for it out of poverty, means that the most powerless are still being the most exploited. If a system only pushes money in one direction, then it's a bad system and one that isn't worth supporting with our dollars. You either buy into the bad system or you choose not to, *if* you have the privilege to do so.

If you have a choice, and you continue to support these systems, ultimately you will hurt the most vulnerable people in it. Because when our money is fired collectively in certain directions it builds very powerful multinational corporations, which become harder and harder to regulate as they scan the world looking for cheap, good labor while demanding lower prices for every deal. With those lower prices always comes exploitation. We saw this when the world began to go into lockdown in February of 2020 due to the spread of COVID-19. Countless brands began to shut down operations, refusing to pick up clothing which had already been produced, and failing to pay factories. We've seen several initiatives to combat this, like the #PayUp campaign. It's pretty rad when people take action. But ultimately what we really need is a system where a multinational corporation worth billions of dollars isn't allowed to do this ever again. We need legislation that protects workers from this happening to them. The system failed its workers.

THE WALMART DILEMMA

Let me tell you what happens when Walmart moves to your town and you live in a rural area. My mother is from Mobile, Alabama, and for a long time (until I understood that it wasn't safe for me to drive that far as a Black person in America...still), I used to make the eighteen-hour drive there by myself, breaking it up and spending the night in Asheville, North Carolina. As I traveled down the Eastern Seaboard, I began to notice from my car window the areas where poverty was the highest. And all these drive-by towns always had at least one Walmart. When Walmart moves into your town with their low low prices, every other business eventually falters because it can't compete with the Walmart prices. The family-owned and -run stores you love close their doors. The independent grocer gives up. Before you know it, entire strip malls look more and more empty. When all these little businesses close their doors because they can't compete with their new massive neighbor, there's less variety available for you, and there's less homegrown industry and retail that brings income and money to you and your neighbors, because there are fewer jobs as well. That's what monopolies do. They work as giant sponges that soak up everything around them. They give us less choice, while limiting access and resources and extracting money from these towns and sending it to the big corps.

On top of this, Walmart and other big corporations often pay their employees very low wages, a fact that has been well documented including in a report by Thomas Buckley on Bloomberg.com. And because they're massive employers in welfare states especially in America, it leaves many individuals on government assistance (food programs and social programs). The owners of Walmart are one of the wealthiest families in the world according to Investopedia.com, yet Walmart pays its staff some of the lowest wages. According to a study by the United States Government Accountability Office commissioned by Bernie Sanders: "Walmart and McDonald's are among the top employers of beneficiaries of federal aid programs like Medicaid and food stamps." These employees depend on government assistance, and who do you think foots the bill for that? Taxpayers like you and me (yes, I pay taxes in both the US and the UK...paying taxes is a good thing but it'd be better if the ultra-wealthy paid their fair share).

Bernie Sanders has discussed this at length, and his office issued a statement in November 2020 saying, "With the individual wealth of high-ranking executives and members of billionaire families like the Waltons, who own Walmart, soaring even as front-line, minimum wage employees and their families struggling to stay afloat amid the devastating Covid-19 pandemic...the stark contrast should be a wakeup call for those who have refused to see how unjust and economically backward it is for the federal government, meaning taxpayers, to subsidize the cruel wages that massive profitable companies force their workers to accept."

Every time you put your money into a big brand, and you have other options (because not everyone does), you're looking the other way on the system that's going to put that independent retailer out of business, leaving less variety and choice and fewer better-paying jobs for everyone. If you can't sell your product (and intellectual property) at a fair price as an independent brand because the big brand (corporation) has undercut you on your own designs and your price, you can't pay your bills and keep your lights on. Lawsuits for copyright theft are notoriously challenging to fight (many have tried and failed). They take a lot of hard cash, emotional outlay, and time, and most independent brands just don't have any to spare (remember that bit about paying people a wage and operating on razor-thin margins).

Just as a big brand like Walmart moves into town and puts the independent retailer out of business, that's essentially what happens in the fashion world, too. The big brands leave little to no room for the small brand to survive. They own the monopoly on that industry. And then there's less variety and choice and fewer jobs. The money goes to the few and not the masses, and that is why the richest twenty-two dudes in the US have more money than all the women in Africa or, according to Oxfam International, the world's 2,153 billionaires have more wealth than the 4.6 billion people who make up 60 percent of our planet. To be even more reductive, the rich really do get richer.

When you choose to shop local and independent, whether it be the corner store (doesn't have to be fancy) or a niche brand, you are sending your money in different directions. Think of it like the blood vessels in your body, the arteries being the corporations and the capillaries and veins being the independents. The whole body can't remain alive if the blood is only pumping through the arteries; it needs to diversify into the whole body through smaller vessels, which allows the oxygen to flow throughout our entire being rather than just our vital organs—it's the smaller communities that feed into the bigger economy. The independent corner shop means that you're keeping your money in your neighborhood, and ultimately that's good for you because your community thrives. Our local corner shop was a real lifesaver for finding flour when the world went into lockdown; it was like the secret hiding spot. But there's also real benefit for you, too. Joanne O'Connell in the *Guardian* reported in 2013: "Research on spending by local authorities shows that for every £1 spent with a small or medium-sized business 63p stayed in the local economy, compared to 40p with a larger business." In the US, per the United States Small Business Association, forty dollars out of every hundred dollars spent at a small local business gets put back into the local economy—whereas only fourteen dollars out of every hundred dollars spent at a big box store comes back to the local economy. The Polish sweater maker in Germany who hires older women she knows to knit her sweaters is supporting a small corner of the world that doesn't often see an influx of money.

When we're not in a global pandemic, local businesses serve as community gathering spaces, which of course builds a stronger community and a network of infrastructure and commerce. Plus local businesses are just pretty cool. That cute artisanal coffee shop that I sometimes get my chai latte from once gave me a lovely loaf of sourdough bread for free because it was closing time and, unlike some corporations, they weren't going to just dump it in the trash when they could give it to a valued customer instead. (Food waste is a massive problem on a global scale and, just as with fashion, we can probably take a stab at who the biggest culprits are.)

Independent and local businesses often reward regulars in ways you never see in big corporations. I mean, in case you haven't noticed, many reward programs are designed just to make you shop more. Example: that big name fast fashion brand, whose in-store "recycling program" presents you with a coupon *so you can buy more clothes*, is actually the problem. It's not quite the same thing as that sweater maker gifting you a sample dress after you've bought two sweaters from her.

We can keep putting our money collectively into a system that we already know is hurting many, or some of us can make a choice—a choice to avoid supporting this system in any way possible (from the intersection you're at, of course, but recognizing where you're at before you claim poverty, because that mindset keeps this system churning, and it involves recognizing your privilege and whether you are "poor" instead of "broke").

HOW DO WE MAKE CHANGE AND WHERE DO WE START?

Brace yourself for having to decide where you want your money to go before you start spending it. After Philip Green (who also used to own Topshop) decided to leave BHS (British Home Store) employees fighting for their retirements because he sold their company for £1 because it was losing money and he wanted to be rid of it, I decided I could never buy his Topshop clothes again. Nothing good can come from anything run by a rich man who happily rips off those with so much less. And anytime I felt the longing, the pull, the call, I remembered the photo of his massive super-yacht (another environmental disaster right there, in addition to his retail activity...much of which is now owned by ASOS), and this visualization of my money going into landing someone I didn't like very much another enormous yacht to pollute the Earth with helped a lot. It quickly helped to erase my need to consume a dress I thought was "nice" for a hot second.

But by taking that pause, I began to realize that my urge to consume soon dissipated if I just took a breath for air. That's also why online transactions for certain stores are made *so super easy*—because researchers for big brands know this. They minimize click-throughs and speed up the buying process in order to keep our endemic short-termist consumer minds satiated. They want to keep our rational and thoughtful purchasing minds at bay for as long as possible by offering add-on purchases, with offers for discounts or free shipping if we spend over a certain threshold, as well as targeting us with other items we may like. They're well aware that the triggers that make us buy compulsively can very easily be thwarted if our attention is lost for a moment.

And don't get me started about looking at an item on a site and having it follow you around the internet, haunting you until you purchase it to just get it to go away. Yummy cookies!

The future looks both bright and bleak. In order for us to live in a future we want, power from some of these brands that haven't been doing things correctly or fairly for a long time has to be redistributed. We—you and I—do that by simply refusing to buy from them when we have other choices available to us. Although no one wants to see folks become jobless, us buying into a system that sucks and kills people will never be the answer. Sadly, it's often everyday folks who lose with these systems in the end regardless. When Topshop was sold to ASOS in 2021, thousands lost their employment seemingly overnight.

People always ask me for brand recommendations, but to be honest that shouldn't be the first thing in the solution tool box so much as investigating your consumption all day, every day. We gotta slow this system down—now—immediately. So first you have to fight the urge to be a consumer, and instead focus more on being a citizen—that's an Orsola de Castro–ism; Castro is the founder of Fashion Revolution. (Plus, I don't want to answer five hundred messages a day advising people on brands and telling people where to shop all day every day when that's a skill set that you should be paying someone for. Instead of devaluing the labor of others with messages seeking free shopping help, go hire a stylist: there are some great ones out there who specialize in sustainable brands, including myself when I'm not really busy.)

Ultimately the market is growing, with the UK parliament's Environmental Audit Committee report "Fixing Fashion" giving estimates that "by 2030 global apparel consumption could rise by 63 percent, from 62 million tons today to 102 million tons—equivalent to more than 500 billion additional T-shirts." The report goes on to say, "Concurrently, soaring demand for apparel—much of it from developing nations—will see the annual retail value of apparel and footwear reach at least €2 trillion by 2030 (an over 30 percent increase of €500 billion between now and then)." In order to curb a growing market, which will further build on exploitation, we have to decrease the demand. That ultimately looks like just buying less.

> "In order to curb a growing market, which will further build on exploitation, we have to decrease the demand."

There is this notion that in order to do more in this conversation, you have to run out and buy the $300 super-ethical dress. That's ridiculous, because you're trying to solve overconsumption with more consumption. And, let's face it, it's a hard jump to make if you're used to paying twenty dollars and getting ten dresses instead of two or three.

So let's just start with:

- slowing down and chilling the fuck out with your wallets and credit cards
- or perhaps just committing to wearing the clothes in your wardrobe for longer (I'm talking years)
- or perhaps committing to buying nothing new for a length of time; I'm proud of you!
- or perhaps committing to thinking about repairing that garment (even if it's fast fashion) that has developed a hole, instead of throwing it away or recycling it; you're in a much better place than the person who displays their entire sustainable wardrobe but doesn't share the part about bagging up trash bags full of fast fashion and dumping them on a charity's doorstep.

If you do just a few steps (and you're not lying to yourself about whether or not you truly do those things, because sometimes we convince ourselves that we're doing something like wearing our clothes until they fall apart when it's pretty clear that the vast majority of us aren't; otherwise it wouldn't be an environmental problem), you're already engaging in a meaningful and helpful way.

HOW DO YOU FIND THE MOST ETHICAL AND SUSTAINABLE GARMENT EVER?

What do you buy next, when you really actually need something?

- Focus on why you should support an independent business instead.
- Focus on the brands that tell you about their company and show you the work that they do in their communities and for the people who make their clothes.

- Consider whether you know this business well, or have just developed brand loyalty because you like the product and the marketing.
- Get to know a new business, instead of buying in the dark, before you devote yourself with total and utter loyalty. Don't be afraid to ask questions.
- Ask a brand if they are striving to pay above living wage (personally, I think we've set the bar too low with a living wage for what we know is backbreaking labor, especially since the living wage is very low in traditionally pillaged countries).
- Ask about the breakdown of their company. Is this a brand that practices diversity in their marketing only? Or are there actual opportunities for people of different ethnicities, genders, and abilities within their corporate offices?
- Ask them not just about their policies but how they plan on implementing them. Nothing turns me off more than a brand that, say, markets a feminist message, but then has an entire board of directors that looks homogenous and very... white man–centric.

When I commit to buying from a small business, I get on up in there. I read about them. I learn about them and read articles about them. Instead of spending hours of my life scrolling a website looking at dress after dress, I've replaced that with hours spent learning about debates around different fibers and dyeing processes. I set internet alerts on the topics I want to learn more about within the fashion supply chain. I don't just judge brands on the garments they're producing but also on how they treat others around them. Do they answer comments on social media in a thoughtful way? Do they take criticism in a thoughtful way? Are they not afraid to join a conversation about racism and diversity in a genuine way, which may not be popular with customers who aren't there yet? Those are the businesses that get my money first these days.

Is this brand more than a business? I ask myself. A corporation can of course act like a person in a court of law, but ultimately it isn't. So when a brand is faced with opposition and they throw tantrums and handle it badly, instead of listening and engaging thoughtfully, I'm rolling my eyes a bit because, mate, you're an entity, not an individual, quit whining and do more. Oh, you don't like it? Well, boo hoo, I don't like living on a planet that keeps heating up gradually by the year.

WHAT ABOUT ENVIRONMENTAL IMPACT?

It's important to note that, when it comes to environmental impact, small and independent brands (especially local businesses) are ultimately always doing less environmental damage than the big box stores, simply because of their size. The small, sustainable brand Lora Gene (with which I am affiliated) is never going to compete with H&M—not on a global scale, but not even in the same ballpark when it comes to planetary harm, because Lora Gene currently has under a hundred styles of clothing in her entire business, while a quick scan at H&M's website in the UK reveals over 7,000 pieces currently for sale (and that's *just* women's clothing…there's menswear, children's wear, and home products on there, too). Fashion brands are notoriously secretive about the volumes of clothing they produce annually, but estimates from Fashion Revolution's 2020

Fashion Transparency Index suggest that around one quarter of the industry's resources are wasted as leftovers. They found that only 27 percent of brands publish information about the steps they are taking to reduce this waste (clothing and textiles, such as "off-cuts, unsold and defective stock, and production samples"). There is an endemic problem with overproduction, added to which there is horrific overconsumption: in the UK alone, 300,000 tons of clothes were thrown away in 2016. In the US, per Remake stated that "The US alone sends 21 billion pounds of textile waste to landfills every year" I suspect that if we knew the true scale of the waste, we'd most likely riot in the streets. But suffice to say that that independent designer who has under a hundred garments for sale on their website naturally has a smaller carbon footprint than the massive multinational corporation that has over a thousand. The person who manufactures a bit closer to home doesn't have a garment flying on five different planes before it reaches the sales floor or the buyer's hands. That in itself makes a huge difference.

People always ask me about the different certifications that exist in the fashion industry. Certifications can be awesome! But please keep in mind that these certifications *only* exist because of the ways in which multinational corporations have behaved for so long, manufacturing in thousands of different factories, thousands of miles away from their headquarters, with little to no input on how those garments are produced, and the human and environmental consequences. The independent brand that uses a handful of small factories, and makes a handful of products, can't always apply certain certifications to what they're doing as a business, but they're also just not doing the same amount of damage. It's all in the scale. Make sure you understand who really needs to be verified and certified in that sort of way.

WHAT ABOUT REGULATION?

Ultimately, we should be staying on top of our governments to regulate these industries. It's a bit like the wild, wild West right now, and anything goes. We put too much trust in brands and corporations to regulate themselves, instead of asking lawmakers to step in and step up. In the words of my good friend Samata Pattinson, the CEO of Red Carpet Green Dress, "Brands are marking their own homework." Would you trust a shark to regulate eating humans? I mean, the shark needs to survive, too, but would you want to be eaten? Neither would I. The market isn't a self-correcting thing. You have to remember that a corporation can only act in its own best interest. If environmental destruction stands in the way of making a higher profit margin for investors, well, you need to keep those investors happy in order for your corporation to stay afloat. And that usually means putting the environment (and other humans) after profit. Being aware of all of this means we can't just sit back and wait for brands to go self-regulate for the better good—"Oh, hey, everyone, this time we're really going to stop harming the environment"—especially because in most cases that would look like making less stuff, caring about how it's made and about the humans who make it, and paying humans better, and that, you guessed it, means much, much smaller profit.

A fashion business that is truly equitable for everyone involved does not make billions in profit, because their profits are more evenly distributed to everyone (farmers, fabric producers, garment workers, production managers, designers at all levels, retail workers, end-of-life management...everyone). Right now that's not happening—not for the garment workers, and not for many who work within the fashion industry (with its current low- to zero-hour salaries, which are a barrier to participation).

As the Union of Concerned Researchers in Fashion manifesto has routinely pointed out: "[W]e need to conduct ourselves in new ways." Similarly, Elizabeth Cline mentioned in conversation with the Sustainable Fashion Forum on the subject of "The Myth of Ethical Consumerism" that, when it comes to "ethical consumerism under capitalism," "I think what people mean, when they say that, is that our only choices are ethical consumption or a revolution to overthrow capitalism, [but] my story is arguing that in fact we have a range of other options besides that." I couldn't agree more.

I don't believe we are going to change these companies to make them entirely better by telling them we are mad at them (but that also hasn't stopped me, because I've got that platform, so why not). But I do think they will change themselves in order to compete with the smaller brands who are doing things better. Instead of championing the race to the bottom (aka a buyer at a fast fashion brand talking the factory down to the lowest possible price), I'm going to champion the brand who's actually doing the best for everyone within the supply chain. That, to me, is more admirable. And I think in order to get there, we have to really change public opinion. We've valued so much bad stuff for far too long. That doesn't make us bad people necessarily, but there are a lot of bad systems that we consistently turn away from acknowledging, because for a long time our society put a lot of value in constant consumption, to the detriment of both people and the planet.

Let's value those things less.

While consistently championing those who just do more.

WHY WE PURGE AND HOW TO STOP THE URGE

The constant need to consume is built off the back of you, the consumer, and your lack of awareness about your habit, and the need you have built inside you to chase a better and improved version of yourself, which you can then project to the world. You want to be recognized by the system, you want to fit in, without realizing you are very much part of the systemic problem.

Additionally, behavioral psychologists see patterns in how we shop and the success of fast fashion. In the article "Is Fast Fashion an Addiction" on voguebusiness.com, behavioral scientist and entrepreneur Matt Wallaert explains, "People have two basic needs for psychological well-being." These are to feel like we're special and unique in some way, but also to feel like we fit in. Keeping up with current fashion trends is one way for people to feel that crucial sense of belonging, while also maintaining individuality through a personal sense of style. It's that fundamental need that the fast fashion industry has gotten good at capitalizing on, Wallaert argues, by accelerating the pace at which the latest trends are replaced. "The business model of consumption is making you feel bad, and then selling you something to make you feel better."

Once I began to sit and think on this, I started to break free of the systems I had been trapped by. In fact, I realized just how trapped I was by fast fashion.

Fast consumption. Fast living. Fast spending. I was buying because I was happy. I was buying because I was sad. I was buying because I wanted certain people to like me. I was buying to fill emotional voids. I was buying because everyone else was. I was buying because I didn't know how to stop. I was buying because I was being constantly bombarded with messaging telling me to buy! Buy! Buy!

This is how people in poverty get trapped by the system. If you're never able to buy the right thing and always have to settle for the thing that will do because of the price divide, often your replacement has a short shelf life, but the quality item is too much for you to afford. So you have to buy bad products again and again. You're stuck in the consumption cycle that you can't afford to get out of. Terry Pratchett's boots theory in *Men at Arms* is useful: "He earned thirty-eight dollars a month plus allowances. A really good pair of leather boots cost fifty dollars. But an affordable pair of boots, which were sort of OK for a season or two and then leaked like hell when the cardboard gave out, cost about ten dollars."

People with disposable incomes are trapped, too. Our middle- and upper-class society just doesn't notice it as much because we're burning through our money but not being forced to make actual *sacrifices*. Sacrifices like "do I pay this electricity bill?" or "do I buy these cheap shoes for work that will only last two months?"

And then those of us with more buying privilege confuse the way the system has made us "broke" with what we think of as "poverty," when the two aren't the same. You can still keep your electricity. You may not have much saved, but that is because you gave a good portion of it to a billionaire company (or at least I know I did once upon a time). And they designed the system where you felt you had to. That you wanted it this way. One time I tallied up all my receipts from fast fashion for the year, and I was legit furious with myself, because I had spent thousands of dollars without noticing, when I took home $12,000 that year (another year living with the parents). It was almost 10 percent of my income.

We all know that there are privileges and barriers to how you're allowed to interact with this system. But it is time for you to understand that if you're above a certain socioeconomic line, you may very well have way more power than you think you do. Sure, it might be easy to throw your hands in the air and say, "It is what it is" or "I am the way I am," but perhaps you don't even like the system as much as you've been told to, and perhaps you've had your fill of the short-lived yet pleasurable rush of dopamine that comes from buying something because you were raised in a consumerist society and now you're looking for something more long-term. Something more meaningful? Something that actually cares for you, and doesn't want to rob you of your future savings, and looks after *your* best intentions?

URGE/PURGE EXERCISES

Look at everything you know about privilege and power and how it works in this world, and ask yourself who you are and where you fall in that system. Remember there's willfully looking away from a system that you know is bad but which you continue to prop up. (Even though you don't like how it affects the community, you personally need the adrenaline rush.)

Now ask yourself, how would you be happier if you stopped purging on fast fashion?

_____

_____

_____

_____

_____

Write down what your urges tell you before you purge:

_____

_____

_____

_____

How do you feel when you receive an email advertising a SALE?

_____

_____

_____

_____

How do you feel when you donate clothes, if it happens more than once a year?

_____

_____

_____

_____

_____

Have you ever lied about the amount of clothing you were buying?

_____

_____

_____

_____

What these exercises flag is how much we dislike the system of constant consumption. Many of us won't miss those impulse buys, because they are usually a Band-Aid for something else we feel at that moment of purchase. We can't purchase a better date or a job interview, or change that shitty day into a great one. So these impulse items inevitably turn out to be failed purchases that hang unhappily in your closet, constantly taunting you and reminding you of the mistake you made when you just needed to take a breath, find some acceptance, and realize that this wasn't going to add to your life, just your closet.

The system of constant consumption feeds into our insecurity and anxiety. That can happen when we feel constantly pressured to participate in a system that smells kind of foul. Yes, choice can be fantastic, but too much of anything isn't good for anyone, as it leaves you with the paradox of choice. You are literally immobilized by the sheer amount of consumables you should consume. So you consume a lot and cheaply, aka those good deals where you bought ten pieces for $200 but in actuality you bought eight pieces that you truly didn't need or want. It's a full-time job to look at thousands of products on websites. It's a full-time job to feel like you have to replace your clothes in order to update the version of yourself you want to become.

But here is the catch: the system will no longer stay massively profitable when people like you and me, who have the privilege of choice, actively decide to stop partaking in the cycle of constant consumption. And when these systems no longer turn over billions of dollars a year in profit...they lose the power they have with governments in our society. We can't and shouldn't expect people without privilege to take down the bad systems, because they don't have the choice we do. It's on us (you, me, and any person with disposable income). This requires everyone to be paid fairly and treated fairly, from those in the supply chain to those buying the clothes, with the ultimate aim of an eradication of poverty.

Even if we're moving in the direction of believing that there's no such thing as ethical consumption under capitalism, you still can't deny that when you give your money to those who abuse power—even though there are other choices available to you and your income, more equitable choices to boot, and yet you're still okay with giving your hard-earned money to someone who directly profits from and enables a bad system—all you're left with are clothes that you didn't even want until an email spammed you and created a sense of urgency in you to buy. Perhaps not...

The point of this chapter and the exercises in it is to get you to start cross-examining and thinking more deeply about your relationship with your consumption, and to realize that in many cases a person who is truly poor couldn't spend in the way you do. They just don't have the luxury of choice. And we are the ones who can break this urge-purge system. Truthfully the system has not just made us broke, but it has broken us, too.

WHERE TO START UNPACKING YOURSELF (AND THE YEARS OF SHIT YOU'VE BEEN TOLD)

Are you feeling overwhelmed by all the information you learned in the first half of the book? Join the club. It's never going to be a good time to discover that the systems of the world disproportionately harm certain groups of people more than others, is it?

The minute I began to understand that all those creeping feelings I had about my own outsized consumption in the past added up to a global and humanitarian crisis, I also felt deep discomfort and guilt. Suddenly, when I saw that £20 dress that would take me countless hours to attempt to mimic on my own sewing machine, I understood its affordability for me meant that someone had been exploited much further down the chain. I felt pretty uncomfortable with that £20 dress and the ones I had bought in the past, too.

I felt silly for not knowing.

I felt silly for claiming I bought those clothes because I was poor when I frankly wasn't...I was just broke from buying too many of those clothes.

I felt bad.

But what we have to realize first is that discomfort is normal when you grow. It's kind of just like exercise. We live in a society in which people treat discomfort and hurt as the same thing, when they're not the same at all. It's not good to hurt people. But separate hurt from discomfort, and recognize that if you're in a position of power and someone with less power tells you about your actions and how it harms them...you're not hurt, you're just feeling discomfort. For example, if a Black person talks to you frankly about race in a way that doesn't center your comfort, it may be uncomfortable but it doesn't hurt you. It instead forces you to recognize privilege and power and who has always held that power in our societies, which feels uncomfortable because those are some hard truths to swallow. And I like to believe, call me Pollyanna, that most people don't wish to move through the Earth hurting others when they have the power to stop.

White supremacy isn't about whether you're a good or bad person; it's a system that we should destroy at all costs. But also recognize that if you are white, we in the West live in a world where whiteness is the default, and it is often associated with goodness. And accept that it is uncomfortable to learn this, but it doesn't hurt you.

Regardless of what you are blind to, it never feels good to learn that you're a part of a system that hurts others and you didn't even realize it. And while that discomfort sucks, it's not going to kill you or even hurt you. But these systems actually do kill other people, and that matters much, much, much more. When a building collapses on people in a traditionally pillaged country because many of us buy into a system that doesn't question why they're being paid such low wages and forced to work in such difficult conditions, we have to face up to the fact that in a small way we allowed it to happen, because we didn't stop doing what we wanted.

11

HOW TO BREAK THE SUPPLY CHAIN

First and foremost, we have to center the voices that need to be amplified most. When it comes to the fashion industry, we have to center makers, particularly garment workers.

No one can advocate for garment workers like they can advocate for themselves, and they're already doing so in groups such as:

Global Fund for Women
Clean Clothes Campaign
Asia Floor Wage Alliance
Labour Behind the Label
The Garment Worker Center
Garment and Allied Workers Union in North India

It's up to us to amplify, give money, time and attention, and listen and share their stories.

The people who make the clothes have very little power against the corporations they help turn a massive profit for. Workers in Bangladesh have already started working to improve conditions on the ground. And that's where we can step in: collective bargaining power is desperately needed, so it's up to us, you and me, to keep the pressure on the brands by letting them know we care about these issues, and it's their job to make sure *all* garment workers are protected and well paid.

I don't think it's a stretch to say that economic and environmental justice is needed in pretty much every country that manufactures and exports a lot of our goods. In the "Actions Make Movements" episode of the podcast *Remember Who Made Them*, Anannya Bhattacharjee of Asia Floor Wage Alliance and Garment and Allied Workers Union in North India talks about consumer action: "The power of the consumer is huge. The brands really fear reputational risk, so they do not like it when it becomes public that their purchasing practices are causing so much exploitation and misery, and when it is well documented, especially when there are examples."

So remember her words next time you're deciding whether or not to buy something you want on a whim, which you probably don't need, which you are pretty sure has been made in dubious circumstances. *The power of the consumer is huge.* Sometimes, when we're trying to walk away but straddling that fence, we will tell ourselves, "Well, what difference does it make?" Turns out, your buying power absolutely does make a difference.

Bhattacharjee explains it: "Brands tend to really get very affected by consumer activism in the home countries, because their market value depends on keeping consumers satisfied. And if you take consumer satisfaction as not just discount prices and low prices but also a belief that the products they consume are produced under fair conditions—if that is one of the parameters of consumer satisfaction—then brands get really affected and fearful of losing the trust of the consumers. I have always said that the consumers in Europe and the United States are extremely important, even if it is one person, five people, ten people, it doesn't have to be a large number. I have seen that the consumer communication to brands, and then the supplier factory also finding out that the brand is agitated by the consumers...The supply chain is such that if the consumer agitates, it vibrates throughout the chain, and it can really bring a lot of pressure onto whatever case we are working on, whatever situation we are trying to correct. So it's a very important voice. And to be in solidarity is extremely important, because time and again we have seen that—keeping a fight very local—for simple things we can get some things done, but for any of the real illegal violations that happen, which happen routinely, the consumer pressure and the brand reaction is very important."

Our job is to keep the heat on and the pressure up.

Direct action does work, whether it's staging your own protest in person or organizing online. This is evidenced by Remake, which did a fantastic job of putting the pressure on brands that canceled their orders and ripped off garment workers during the COVID-19 pandemic, through their #PayUp campaign. But this fight's not over. As of early 2021, many brands still haven't *paid up* when they ceased needing their orders, and even worse during all of this, other brands have renegotiated for better discounts on what were already starvation wages for garment workers. So, this fight is *far* from over.

Agitate the bottom rung of the ladder so the top rung begins to lose its balance and pay attention.

WHY WE CONSUME

Annie Leonard, executive director of Greenpeace, has this to say on *The Story of Stuff*: "Guess what percentage of *total* material flow through this system is still in product or use six months after [its] sale in North America. Fifty percent? Twenty? *No*. One percent. One! In other words, ninety-nine percent of the stuff we harvest, mine, process, transport—ninety-nine percent of the stuff we run through this system is trashed within six months."

Our dependency on stuff and how we consume has not been designed by us, but it is, per Leonard, "the heart of the system, the engine that drives it." That is why it is so important that the corporations protect "the golden arrow of consumption"; this has become a top priority. Leonard says, "That is why, after 9/11, when our country was in shock, President Bush could have suggested any number of appropriate things: to grieve, to pray, to hope. *No*. Bush said to shop. *To shop?!* We have become a nation of consumers. Our primary identity has become that of consumer, not mothers, teachers, farmers, but consumers. The primary way that our value is measured and demonstrated is by how much we contribute to this arrow, how much we consume. And do we!"

This attitude is *not* just limited to the US either, before anyone gets too smug. At the time of my writing this book, the world is still in a global pandemic and fighting against the spread of COVID-19. We have been socially distancing for over a year. However, in June 2020, after several months of isolation and store closures, Prime Minister Boris Johnson relaxed the pandemic restrictions in a bid to get the economy back. In a nutshell, Johnson urged consumers to get back out there and, well, consume. Johnson said publicly, "I think people should shop, and shop with confidence, but they should of course observe the rules on social distancing and do it as safely as possible."

But is that really possible?

Yes, we shop for food in grocery stores because food is a necessity, but did anyone really need a flowy maxi dress for a summer in which, most of us knew, we'd mostly be inside? I'm not a scientist, but I sure do listen to them, and all of them urged against following the advice of the merry trio of male politicians appearing on our screens to give us our daily coronavirus briefings to open up stores and pubs and restaurants and spend, spend, spend.

We saw this again later in the year approaching the holiday season. Stores were open. And then closed again. Every time the stores opened, it would seem the virus spread more quickly, and everything was shut down again. At the beginning of the UK's lockdowns in 2020, I wrote about the retail stores staying open despite the general vibe being "Get off the streets, you clowns." I began to receive messages and tweets from scared retail workers talking about how colleagues were calling in sick and being forced to work anyway or risk losing their employment. Some workers complained that their stores weren't even equipped with hand sanitizer and wipes. Additionally, many workers talked of feeling scared to work because of living with vulnerable family members, and being afraid to ride public transportation to get to said job. All for what? So that billionaires could keep the money flowing upward. It even seemed as though the government and the shops were playing a game of pandemic chicken with each other. The government didn't want to force the stores to close, and the stores didn't want to risk those of us who were willing to brave COVID-19 for a quick adrenaline hit. Eventually, when the furlough scheme—in which the UK government offered to pay 80 percent of employees' salaries during the pandemic—came about, the stores began to close. But many of the chains that are owned by billionaires could have very well made that call on their own.

They *chose* not to.

They had the power to stop.

But that isn't the only time a UK politician has talked about consumers spending their money during a pandemic. In December 2020, Rishi Sunak, the chancellor of the exchequer, said, "I feel good about the bounceback. I think people have been sitting at home, building up some savings hopefully, and we would like to go and spend them when we get back." Yup, you heard it, please can we have the savings you saved during this sad and lonely time (if you were lucky enough to save)? Although the world is looking at a possible recession, and job prospects aren't great right now, we politicians still want you to be as loose and free with your money as before. Next they'll turn around and tell us the reason our generation doesn't own houses is not because our salaries have remained fixed for about two decades, and house prices, even during the pandemic, have gone through such a period of high inflation that they are even now at an all-time high; it's actually because of one too many avocado toasts or something.

Ahhh, it's been a way of life in our society. Let's go back to *The Story of Stuff* (Annie, I owe you a check, or at least a donation to Greenpeace). *The Story of Stuff* talks about the economic recovery of the world after World War II, and how retail economist Victor Lebow came up with a very strong narrative that keeps the wheel going. He said: "Our enormously productive economy... demands that we make consumption our way of life, that we convert the buying and use of goods into rituals, that we seek our spiritual satisfaction, our ego satisfaction in consumption... we need things consumed, burned up, replaced, and discarded at an ever-accelerating rate." *The Story of Stuff* also highlights that Raymond Saulnier, chairman of President Dwight Eisenhower's Council of Economic Advisors, said, "[The American economy's] ultimate purpose is to produce more consumer goods."

Christ.

It would seem many of our politicians think that our thirst for consumer goods, which includes fast fashion, is a quick fix for some of the worst issues ever to take place on this planet. But meanwhile, as we're being urged to continue to buy into a cycle, it is actually harming people. Especially during the pandemic. In October of 2020 an Amazon warehouse in Coventry, England, suffered a COVID-19 outbreak among its workers. And earlier, in July 2020, a clothing factory in Leicester, England, experienced a COVID-19 outbreak as well. In July 2020 the *Guardian* reported that "the trail of the new outbreak led to Leicester's garment industry and the thousands of factories that continued to operate during lockdown, some allegedly without proper social distancing and in squalid conditions. Some of those factories supply the online fashion retailer Boohoo, which has seen a massive backlash this week." In the United States, a meat processing plant in Los Angeles County endured an outbreak of COVID-19, which was just one of many. Per the Food and Environment Reporting Network, "In recent months, as [Los Angeles County] has become a Covid-19 epicenter, in part driven by outbreaks at manufacturing facilities...with over 300 cases reported in January alone."

So we're all supposed to be protecting ourselves and staying home, but also shopping, but also what about the workers who get you those consumer goods? How can they protect themselves? Is it better to have a job without COVID-19, or a job with COVID-19? Why is our society like this? Should people be shopping right now? I can totally see how this messaging could be confusing. That's by design as well.

12

HABITS ARE MADE
TO BE BROKEN

Life is a series of habits.

And humans are creatures of habit.

Think about it. You wake up, brush your teeth, groom yourself, and go to school or work or go about your day. So much of our life is habitual. And those habits can be both good and bad. And while so much of our life can be determined by factors like privileges and advantages, habits play a part in it, too. All of our habits add up to an outcome. And, depending on the habit, the outcome can be good or bad. Habits are also interesting, because often you don't notice their effects until you're aware of the pattern. Knowing how habits work can change your life.

Knowing all this, I now recognize that, for me, buying and consuming fast fashion was a habit more than anything else. And when I look around at many other people who exist on the same socioeconomic playing field as I do (or above), I see those same habits playing out. While I have talked about the ways in which fast fashion consumption preys on our insecurities, I also know that when I made purchases multiple times a month, it was mostly out of habit. I had to break myself out of that cycle in order to feel free again. But it wasn't a cold turkey, quitting sort of thing either. You see, consumption exists in the very fiber of so many societies that it's hard to pry it apart. Consumption is, in a nutshell, completely normalized and systematized. Show me a fun cult classic film with a good leading lady and I'll find a scene where a character in that film is completely transformed with a little makeover magic (often accompanied with a really fun shopping montage: *Pretty Woman*, anyone? "You work on commission? Big mistake! Huge!").

In order to really disentangle yourself from a system (which you're paying into constantly and kinda don't want to), first start out by being realistic with yourself. If you're anything like me, you were probably shopping mostly for the kick that you can only get while making a purchase (even though you knew deep down that you didn't need yet another garment that you would tire of quickly). So when I first began to feel that nagging notion that my shopping wasn't helping anyone—the planet, my wallet, or even myself—I knew that I had to stop, but I knew it would be hard because I was conditioned to shop. After all, we live in a consumerist society that quietly measures your self-worth against...having a lot of stuff.

Sometimes I see these pledges with grand goals like "no new clothes for a year." Rather optimistic, but let's be honest: it's a pretty hard-core challenge for serious consumers. Goals like this set people up for failure. We love to give up after one little slip-up. But ultimately being more thoughtful about your consumption isn't about any sort of goal; it's a lifestyle change, and a way of changing your thought patterns and spending habits. A goal insists that there's some sort of summit to reach, but it should be about long-term striving and pledging toward change, which is a pretty consistent practice. I never challenge people to any specific length of time, mostly because the concept is daunting to people, and different folks have different needs. The person who is plus size doesn't have as many clothing options as a person who is standard size. If you only have two pairs of really good work trousers and one pair gets busted beyond repair...you're going to need to buy some, and often there are not a wealth of ethical or sustainable options immediately within reach. But I also find that if you don't challenge people with a specific length of time, many times, after reading the facts and the figures, they'll unconsciously start to challenge *themselves* without even a prod.

Often I receive messages that go something like: "Hi, Aja, when I first found you, I was uncomfortable with it because I enjoyed buying a lot of stuff (but I didn't really think it was that much at the time). I basically thought I would never change. Then one day I began to think about it and thought I'd take a week off from shopping. One week turned into a month. One month turned into three months. I'm now six months in and I'm horrified looking back at how much I was *actually* buying. Surprisingly, I now realize I'm saving more money than before, and I'm frustrated that I didn't slow down a little sooner."

Yup. That's how I felt, too. But I started slowly. I started only with shifting my mindset. This helped me to realize that the amount of clothing I bought actually did stress me out deep down inside, though I probably wasn't ready to acknowledge that to myself.

The problem is, when you're still caught up in the cycle, you try to rationalize your decisions as normal. One little dress can't hurt (except you don't need it and you're buying it several times a month, and it adds up to several problems...but you don't really notice because the RRP isn't *that* much, and you really wanted it, although you didn't until you saw it being worn on Instagram by someone who is paid to wear it so that you will be influenced enough to buy it).

And sometimes labels really matter, whether we realize it or not. It served me well to remind myself, whenever I felt the urge to shop: "I don't actually like fast fashion." Because for so long, I had identified as a fast fashion consumer in my head. This was the label I had given myself. But once I began to change my sense of identity, I found it easier to change my buying habits as well. Consumer buying habits actually shift economies. If we live in a society that tells us we are what we own, think about how powerful that can be in shifting mindsets and priorities. Your consumer identity is representative of what you want to be in life and how you want others to see you, too. Kelly Peeler of NextGenVest said on the *Bad with Money with Gaby Dunn* podcast episode "Screaming into a Jar (aka Student Loans)," "Number one: Primary leading indicator of a consumer financial crisis is a change in consumer identity." But what if a change in consumer identity could be used to predict that *good* things were coming your way instead? What if it were an indicator of more of us winding down and stepping back from consumption? I believe that how you choose to identify is linked to who you *want* to be, which has a lot more potency over your consumer identity and profile. If you step back from any outdated identifications, you will be that one bit freer from the addictions that enabled you to get here.

In my case, I constantly reminded myself that I enjoyed

the things in my closet that I had saved for dutifully and wore proudly. Instead of telling myself that I was a fast fashion consumer, I told myself that I was a person who saved and cherished my clothes and treated myself with the same worth. In the past, I viewed myself as a person who could *only* buy fast fashion (because, let's be honest, there were years when my annual salary was pretty low despite my other privileges), but once I began to positively assure myself that I didn't need to buy three dresses every time I entered a store, I felt a seismic shift. I soon found that I actually did have the money for that ethical designer, and it only took a month or two to save for it. I also liked myself more as a result. I felt better about the value I had ascribed as the owner, wearer, and carer of the garment. I simply began to value my clothes more. It felt more caring and fulfilling all around.

I had less, but I was happier with what I had.

YOU CAN'T BUY YOURSELF ETHICAL

I can't say this enough. You can't really buy your way to being more sustainable. Spending all your money on being the most "ethical" and the most "sustainable" is utterly counterproductive and brings us back to...the endemic problem, which is that we are programmed to right wrongs as a consumer, not a citizen, when what we need more of is less. To be more ethical we need to uproot our consumer self and plant the seeds for slow growth and less accumulation through caring for what we have and for the world around us.

To have less and to want less won't happen overnight, and it won't be a "swipe to ethical lifestyle." So much of how we live now in our fast consumption cycle has programmed us with the need for instant gratification. Everything we are sold and told is a quick fix, shortcut, two weeks to zero waste, I could go on…This has left us with a real sense of endemic short-termism: real change is slow and accumulative. And it needs fostering and caring for. Just as you wouldn't expect a bulb you have planted to grow overnight, nor will sustainable, organic, and in-line-with-the-planet ethical living.

It took me well over a year to pare down. I recycled my stuff through Craigslist, FreeCycle, Facebook, friends…if you can use it, you can have it. And every time I go back to the US I make sure I do this with the stuff I left at my parents' house, too, since I want to unburden them of my consumerist mistakes. When you have spent time trying to right the wrong of your accumulation, it makes you consider much more rigorously why you need to acquire new stuff. I often think about how we will all leave this Earth for the next realm. And when I do, I don't want to leave behind piles of crap that someone else is burdened with sorting through. I want the items I leave behind to be valuable or usable or collectable.

Wow, I took it dark for a moment, but those are the facts. What are we acquiring for? We can't take anything with us, but what we can do on this Earth is leave it in a better state because of our actions to the ones we love and the world we love, too.

MAKE THE MOST OF WHAT YOU HAVE

From my previous years as a dedicated, consummate consumer, I pretty much have shoes for the next ten years. I bought too much, and now I wear them to make good the cost of their creation. I still wear many of my less ethical options, because that's more sustainable than dumping them in someone else's lap and running out to buy the newest sustainable trainers that I don't even need in order to shout to the world about how "sustainable" I am. See the problem here? We need to use what we have right now, even if that means using up and wearing down the things we have brought with us up to this point. The things that aren't ethical can become ethically owned if they are used properly. This is the ethical trap that even ethical retailers seldom tell you about: if you want to do good, use up what you have.

So, here are a few ethical tips that people leave out when they're trying to sell you glass jars to display your zero-waste stuff in. (Chances are, if you are someone who is around or below the poverty line, you're operating from a much more sustainable place than many people. Keep up the good work. The name of the game is surviving. If you're buying five to ten garments of fast fashion a year instead of fifty...you really aren't the problem here.)

1. **Challenge the free t-shirt/tote bag business.** Is your work or school, or an event you're attending, planning on giving away free swag that the receivers will inevitably sleep in? Push back. My friend Liz Ricketts from the OR Foundation is on a "personal mission to eradicate single-use t-shirts" because of what she's witnessed in Kantamanto, Ghana's largest secondhand market.

   Here's what you probably don't know about that free t-shirt you didn't even want, as Liz explains:

   > Most single-use t-shirts function as swag given out for free to commemorate a specific occasion, incentivize a donation, or acknowledge group affiliation. Free means that the cost of production is as low as possible. In short, most novelty (swag) t-shirts are not made with people and the planet in

mind. There is always the argument that people will cherish these items and wear them often, thereby honoring the resources and labor required to make them, but I see almost no evidence of this. And if every event gives out a t-shirt, how can anyone possibly cherish all of those shirts? Most end up as waste.

Oh, but friends, it gets so much worse.

Thrift stores are full of novelty t-shirts. Not only are they one of the most donated items by individuals, but organizations typically order more than they can give away at their events and then donate the excess. It is not uncommon to find barrels with fifty-plus of the same t-shirt in the back warehouse of a charity shop. I know because I make rugs out of them. When they have multiples of something, thrift stores try to avoid oversaturation by staggering when they hang these t-shirts on the rack. Still, t-shirts are often bundled up and offered at a discount 'grab bag' price, because there are simply more than any thrift store can sell.

Guess how many of these t-shirts end up in Kantamanto? The OR's research finds that roughly 25 percent of shipping containers received in Kantamanto are t-shirts that were given away for free, which is more than any other clothing item received. If we don't want it, do you think the sellers and buyers of Kantamanto do?

And sometimes the t-shirts have been printed three months prior (if they're for an event, they're often dated). And often that t-shirt actually has a bigger carbon footprint than...you do. It's definitely been on more trips at the end of its life cycle. And we're not even counting the beginning.

Per Liz of the OR, "Within those three months that t-shirt could have been a flop on Depop, donated to one thrift store, sorted, hung on the rack, passed over, sorted again, exported to a bigger thrift store in another state, same process, still passed over, exported to Canada for final sorting, baled up and exported to Ghana before being purchased by a retailer in Kantamanto."

This system is a lose–lose for everyone, and it's pervasive everywhere. I'd argue the free tote bag market probably looks the same. I would love to see people purchasing boxes of free tote bags that weren't used and repurposing them for new events with a little screen-printing magic. How fun would that be? Even a screen-printing booth at the event so you could see how it's made.

But the freebie business is a headache. It's a headache for the event and a headache for you, once you realize you have an item you're ultimately not going to use.

As Liz concludes: "Finally, I will say that this typical life cycle seems to bring little joy to anyone involved. When I talk to organizations about why they order t-shirts, the typical response is, 'I wish we didn't.'"

> Talk to your work.
>
> Your school.
>
> Your charity race.
>
> Your sorority or fraternity.
>
> The world doesn't need more t-shirts.
>
> Especially ones that we don't actually want.

2. **Commit to buying a portion of your wardrobe secondhand.**
It's going to vary, depending on the person and your intersection with what you can buy. I know, I know, I know that accessibility is an issue. The options for plus-size folks are still limited (I know, because I'm looking for myself). It can also be daunting and challenging. But the process of searching for just-right items slows us down in general. Personally, I'd rather wait for that perfect item from the perfect fashion brand secondhand than buy something new from a less than ethical brand. Do you follow @selltradeplus on Instagram? You should. Beautifully curated clothes priced fairly and all secondhand. But they're not the only ones. There are new accounts like this popping up every day, and it brings me joy to see secondhand markets slowly becoming more inclusive. If you're looking to begin your journey, shopping a more curated feed is a great way to dip your oar in, in a low-stress way. *Soon you'll be ready to graduate to eBay.*

But it isn't just eBay these days. You've got Vestiaire Collective, The RealReal, thredUP, Depop, Vinted, Poshmark. And by the time I finish writing this, I'm sure there will be even more options. As FashionUnited reported in 2020, "The U.S. secondhand clothing market is projected to more than triple in value in the next 10 years—from 28 billion dollars in 2019 to 80 billion dollars in 2029."

3. **Be mindful of how you shop.** People without means have been doing this all along, so keep that in mind. If you're a secondhand seller, be careful that the way you source isn't displacing those who rely on secondhand clothing to dress themselves. It's all about thinking about the other person here.

I get asked a lot about the gentrification of thrifting. I always thought the question sounded a little off the mark, knowing good and well that the world overproduces clothing and that's the largest hurdle for this entire system. Is that Depop seller displacing you? Most likely no, when we know how much clothing ends up being sent to the Global South. Your charity shop sucks now, simply because there's more fast fashion and the quality of clothes has gone massively downhill in the last twenty years. But the gentrification of thrift is *not* new, because the Global North has always skimmed the best bits from the top before dumping everything else in the Global South. I think it's a developing conversation, to be honest. I haven't personally read much yet in a scientific way about the popularity of thrifting and how it affects those who are more marginalized. The truth is there's *a lot* of clothing on planet Earth. So the more that gets recycled, the better, and the higher the prices that secondhand clothing commands, the more this industry will profit, which will be a move toward more ethical capitalism. The concern is that the people who rely on cheap secondhand clothes are priced out of this model, but the more value that is placed on good-quality clothes, the more the markets will wake up to the fact that clothing needs to be affordable (by tighter margins, smaller mark-ups, smaller profits for billionaire owners and stakeholders)—but also fair trade, high-quality, and more for the garment worker. In some ways, this will stop the trap that is fast fashion that you can't afford to buy your way out of.

As far as the gentrification of thrift goes, Liz Ricketts has some key points on that conversation, too, to keep in mind:

"The gentrification of thrift is not new. Recognizing this

is key to fostering solidarity between 'modern' resale and 'traditional' secondhand markets like Kantamanto.

"We must remember that the secondhand clothing trade, or thrift, has always been a for-profit venture born of fashion's excess. The people who collect and sort clothing in the Global North are looking to make the most money from each garment as possible. Through the sorting process the Global North skims off the higher quality goods—what is sometimes called the creme, or vintage—whereas the lower quality stuff is exported to the Global South.

"The Global North has been extracting the higher quality stuff for decades while shipping 'inferior' products to 'developing' countries. This is the way the business model works. Again, secondhand is not charity, it is a business and a supply chain."

The system doesn't just affect those of us in the Global North; it affects the globe. Ricketts adds, "Often this is with the best intentions, but it's worth noting that in his book *Clothing Poverty*, Andrew Brooks outlines some pretty shady charity licensing practices, where charities essentially sell their name to for-profit secondhand businesses."

It's good to be aware when we're unpacking our saviorism that we're not being *so* very charitable dumping the stuff we didn't need to buy on someone else's doorstep.

4. **Buy smart.** If you're going to buy discounted merchandise, here's the thing: don't ask annoying questions about it being fake to a seller who has 100 percent perfect feedback and is selling the thing you want for the best price you're ever going to get at that moment in time...because they won't sell to

you. (Also, no one who is selling a fake handbag is ever going to be like, "Why yes, this bag is fake, why do you ask?")

Instead, learn how to authenticate goods yourself. Here are some tips:

Does the person sell a range of items, or do they just appear to have hundreds of that one particular bag (for example)?

Does the bag have store tags from an actual department store? Generally, counterfeit goods don't take this step.

Is it too cheap? No one's letting you have an in-demand bag for 90 percent off. Get real.

Do some independent research. There are a slew of YouTube videos out there that will tell you everything you need to know about the bag and what to look for. Don't forget to like and leave a nice comment on the video. They just did the labor for you.

Rest assured most online platforms have safety nets in place. PayPal will often hold money until the seller accepts the purchase. In that time, you can check it over, and if it doesn't sit right with you, you can open a case on eBay.

Think about why you're really buying this item. Are you buying it because you truly love it, or are you buying it because all the cool people have it?

5. **Borrow/swap with a friend.** Our bodies change shape, and that is a normal part of being human. However, the way our society talks about weight gain is problematic. How about:

"Hey, so-and-so, you recently said that all your clothes felt a little too tight, as do mine. Instead of buying new things, why don't you take my size XX trousers instead? They're too snug for me." Let's normalize talking about changing size, rather than rushing out to buy all new clothes.

6. **Just wear your clothes.** No, really. A survey of 2,000 women in 2015 by Censuswide for Barnado's showed that the average person in the UK wears their clothing *seven* times. I know it sounds shocking, but I remember a time period where maybe that was me for some of the items I was buying (probably because some of them didn't last longer than five wears...).

Now, if I'm considering buying an item, I ask myself if I intend to wear it a hundred times.

But also, will this garment last a hundred wears?

If the answer is no, I walk away.

7. **Take good care of your clothes** (so they last a long time). Learn how to mend things. Or, if that's not your thing, take them to a dry cleaner. But at least learn how to sew a button back on! It's not hard at all (there are hundreds of videos demonstrating how). When I get nice shoes with soft soles, I take them to the cobbler immediately and have them put a rubber sole on so they'll last a long time. I waterproof shoes I love immediately. I only wash my sweaters when they're truly dirty (meaning once a season for some). Wool is naturally antibacterial on its own, because of the lanolin, so it doesn't need a wash after every wear, especially if it doesn't smell. I hand-wash most of my wool sweaters myself, because it's the best way to keep your wool in its best shape.

It is important to know a little about fabric composition when it comes to what clothes you buy and how you intend to care for them. Some fabrics are easy and undemanding but will deteriorate quickly, and others are more hard-wearing but need more maintenance. Which brings us back to the Kantamanto secondhand market in Accra. Liz Ricketts points out: "Ghanaian consumers are far more discerning than the average consumer in the Global North because bespoke tailoring is still commonplace, and most Ghanaians grow up co-constructing their wardrobe—Ghanaians have an intimate understanding of fashion. This means that Ghanaian consumers recognize low-quality construction and materials, whereas many Global North consumers cannot define quality construction and do not know how to discern durability. With this in mind it seems that we should then be sending our highest quality secondhand goods to Ghana where they would surely put them to use."

We could really learn a thing or two from Ghanaian fashion lovers. They seem to know sustainability better than the rest of us...yet they are landed with the stuff we don't want. And these "dead white man's clothes" are filling up their country in landfill and choking their natural resources and environment. You need to see it to believe it—the size of our waste deposited and spoiling their land. Ask yourself, why?

MAKE MORE SPACE FOR YOURSELF AND NOT MORE STUFF

I don't know about you, but I started dancing ballet as an adult of twenty-four, pretty much right when I got home from that weird year in New York City. And when I tell people that I dance ballet as an adult I'm met with faces of total and utter confusion, because we live in a society where people cannot quantify doing things for fun that other people get paid for (unless we count sports). When you live in a consumerist society that doesn't value the labor of others, the idea of doing certain things for fun seems foreign. What is to be gained? And why do you do it if there is no gain?

Somewhere along the line we became a society that championed stuff over hobbies, and hobbies became something limited to the wealthy. But I had to get some hobbies that didn't involve material goods to get over my obsession with buying all this stuff. Distancing myself from the notion that consumption and stuff were entirely tied to my self-worth was a feat, and it wasn't a linear thing either. It didn't happen overnight, it took a matter of years, but I can also say without a doubt that ballet, that hobby I made time for, definitely helped.

You see, privilege is a gray area when it comes to financials. (The Resource Generation website has some helpful qualifiers to ascertain where you fall in this spectrum.) Although my family edged toward middle-class markers, race makes a lot of things...frankly harder and more unstable. So, although my family was privileged in a lot of ways, it didn't feel that way because of where we fit in the invisible but powerful hierarchy. Ballet was one privilege that was always just out of my reach. I had dabbled in dance classes for one school year but, with the time, commitment, and cost, my mother said no more when that year was over. The woman who wasn't going to pay fifteen dollars in the 1990s for a single t-shirt from the Gap wasn't exactly thrilled to pay eighty dollars for our jazz costumes for our recitals. And, let's be honest, that wasn't the only cost. Don't forget the professional photographer who comes around to the studio to photograph all the dancers individually. That's more money. But from that one solid year of dance, I found myself mesmerized with the ballet dancers and asked my parents if next year I could do ballet instead. It was met with a hard no.

But let's go back to BIPOC parents because, although my own didn't exactly tell me, "You have to be a doctor or a lawyer" (two occupations I decided for myself that I would be between the ages of six and ten), they did "want to give our child the tools to success so they can make it in this world, and ballet ain't it." Especially as ballet is notoriously a very white world. There were a handful of Black dancers who were making it work, but the general sense was "this isn't a world that actually wants you." On top of that I started to fill out about age ten, and since the world hates fat bodies and the ballet world still remains pretty fatphobic, my parents decided, "We're not sinking money into this." Let's break down the costs of ballet. Once you graduate to your pointe shoes, you're quickly burning through several pairs a month. Pointe shoes have a limited lifespan (and "die," which means that they're useless and won't support your foot in the way you need it to be supported to execute the moves) because you wear them hard and the sweat from your feet breaks down the glue. Basically, professional ballet dancers can go through ten pairs a week (or more if you're performing a lot). Let's say you, as a trainee, go through four pairs of shoes a month. At sixty dollars a pop and over, that's an extra $240 a month expense for a family. In a year, that's $2,880. While I was disappointed with my parents for a pretty long time,

I definitely get their point. No matter what anyone says, ballet is a privileged kid's sport. There are a few lucky ones who might not have the privilege or money but instead have someone who notices their skill early on and helps them to make it work. But for a lot of kids, without that line item in your parents' budget, it's the dream that's just out of your reach.

And so, when I was twenty-four and decided I would take some ballet classes, I was having one of those twenty-something moments of absolute self-loathing. Nothing in my life was perfect. I never thought I'd meet someone, and my rampant consumerism was not sparking joy. I needed to find my joy somewhere else. I had taken ballet as an elective at university as well because I've always believed that, with school, any time you can take a class that doesn't involve written tests, you should go for it. I took ballet and I loved it. I always knew I would.

Why do I make space for it? I dance because my dance is an act of rebellion. It is an absolute rejection of everything I have been told about my bigger Black body. It is being seen in the loudest way possible while never uttering a word. It empowers some and silences others. It is my personal peace and a good portion of my joy. It is the thing I keep telling myself to quit because I'm getting old and I get more aches and pains than I ever used to... but I can't! And it gives me a much better endorphin rush than the dopamine of fast fashion ever did. And once I realized that, I started to think it was high time to make sure I was pouring more of my money into ballet than fast fashion. It was a decision.

One thing I hear often is "But how do you afford it? It's not cheap!" No, it isn't. Another thing I'm often asked is: "What do you do?," as in "What's your job?" I never knew how to answer that one, because I never really enjoyed my career path until recently, so I started asking people to ask me instead, "What do you like to do?" And often folks looked at me sideways. Serves me right for being a pretentious fuck.

What do you need to make space for? Why don't we start asking people about the things they like, instead of measuring their value by what they do for money? We value people sometimes based off their job choice and their proximity to wealth, and that feels super icky, but we do it without even thinking, especially when we ask about someone's occupation first and foremost. I am now going on fifteen years into ballet. The pandemic changed everything, and I've not been in a studio for more than a year. I was heartbroken for all the professional dancers and trainees of the world whose lives have been turned upside down. But I'm still dancing. At least once a week, while holding on to my table for balance. Because that is what ballet is. It is the thing that has given my life the most amount of balance. Please go find yours. And I am not talking the bank kind.

CHANGE YOUR PATTERN TO CHANGE THE OUTCOME

Often people don't realize that when you're trapped in a bad habit, you need to change your pattern in order to change the outcome. So, keep note of the times when you shop and change those patterns. For me it took avoiding certain stores for a while. It's easier to just not go in, rather than go in and be tempted. It also took (and this is *very* important, so listen carefully) **unsubscribing from *all* the emails and uninstalling all the apps.** Those pesky push emails you get every single day? Surprise!

It's by design. Feeding and flirting with your needs. They target you when you crave them the most. The urgency instilled in you when you see that 50 percent discount that will be offered again before you know it is the same urgency that fuels sites to crash. We have been told to spend but also to save. No wonder we have been programmed to spend/save in droves. That, too, is by design. Without social media and emails I suspect the consumer landscape would look very different. They definitely wouldn't know so much about our impulse drives and when we have the least amount of impulse control. We have played our part in giving them everything they need to know to keep selling to us, even when we don't crave it or want to.

The first thing I did when I began to move into the direction of slowing down was to allow myself fewer clothing items and more beauty products. I couldn't go cold turkey. I needed some drip feed or I would just overspend and overconsume again. So I allowed myself beauty products. And it turns out discount stores are a fantastic place to shop for beauty products because beauty has a shelf life, which means upmarket stores and others clear out their stock semi-regularly. Additionally, if a cosmetic brand decides to change the look of their product or the packaging, perfectly good items get taken off the shelf and sent to a discount retailer in order to keep everything uniform and "on brand" in the store. I began to get really good at rolling up my sleeves and diving into piles of beauty products in order to find that one elusive brand that I had seen in blogs and magazines. And believe it or not, if you keep your eye out, it always turns up. You see, our society operates on overproduction with everything. We simply make too much of all products because retailers would rather have too much, in hope of selling a lot, than too little and risk missing out on a transaction. Until we as a society stop overproducing so much of *everything*, it would serve you well to have a nose around your local discount store, especially if you're looking for a quick kick but not trying to break the bank. It's a small win, too, because the next stop for many of these products is the dumpster and landfill anyway. So, in that way, you're not exactly feeding into the demand.

PAY ATTENTION TO YOUR IMPULSES

Pay attention to when you feel compelled to shop and consciously divert yourself. And my golden rule is this: you're never allowed to go shopping when you're feeling bad about yourself or wearing clothing you don't love. If you go into a shop and you're wearing an outfit you hate and clothing you don't shine in, you'll naturally want everything in the shop in comparison. It's like grocery shopping when you're hungry. Don't do it, because you'll take home the entire pastry aisle (at least I will). When I enter a store, I go dressed in my finest. You will naturally compare the quality of the item on the rack with what you are wearing on your body. If the garment on the rack doesn't match in quality and design, you're much less likely to take it home with you. This rule never fails, and it's saved me from a lot of clothing where the quality didn't match up to the expectations I want for my wardrobe. And for myself.

PAY ATTENTION TO QUALITY

Products made on the fast fashion production line are produced hastily, makers are badly paid, and the quality is poor. Focus on the quality, on the detail and its execution. Look at the fabric, feel it between your fingers, look at the cut and the workmanship. Is it good quality? Feel valuable when you purchase clothes, and you will purchase valuable assets for your wardrobe that will last for a long time.

Fast fashion is like sugar. (And I love sugar...just like I once loved fast fashion.) Living between the UK and the US, I notice the sugar content in foods in the US is much higher than in the UK. I craved sugar when I got off the plane in the UK, but after a few weeks the cravings lessened and I reached a better equilibrium. But when I go back to the US and I order something from a restaurant that I used to eat with regularity, I can really taste the sugar, and sometimes it feels too much. It almost feels sickly and I wonder, how could I not have tasted this before? Fast fashion is similar. When you're in the cycle of consistent buying, you want it all and you want it now, and you're not looking too closely at what you're even consuming because you're addicted. A week or two away from the stores and the apps, and the desire tapers off. You reach a better equilibrium where the product and its producers don't control your addictions. You do.

PAY ATTENTION TO THE ACTIVITY OF CONSUMING

So much of consumption is built into friendships and social activities, we don't even realize it. In order to change certain habits, sometimes it's necessary to change the ways in which you hang out with friends. I had friends in my youth where our only real connection was buying things together at the mall. Once I began to feel uncomfortable with it all, there was a bit of a divide in the friendship. Some people come back, some people don't. When you're young, many of your friendships aren't permanent, and sometimes friendships come to an end. It's better than arguing with someone all day about why you don't want to go shopping.

I lucked out with my best friend. We used to *love* to shop together. It was our social activity. But a few years ago, we both naturally started to drift into a direction of being more mindful. Call it age, call it realizing everything I'm writing about in this book, but something happened where we no longer wanted to consume recklessly together. Instead, we started going to more movies, more museums, having more game nights, and volunteering. True friendships grow together.

I always find clothing items from a certain multilevel-marketing leggings company (who expanded to dresses and other items), and it bugs me because a lot of the stuff is new with tags, which tells me that someone only really made that purchase in the name of friendship and now they've dumped it on a charity shop. And I don't think that's okay at all. Once again, someone in Accra, Ghana, is digging through a trash pile, and there are the leggings you bought because you didn't want to hurt your friend's feelings... polluting someone else's neighborhood.

So think about how you can change the outcome before you purchase. Commit to extricating yourself from things that lead you down one path.

You have control about what happens next.

Just stop a while and think.

13

I BELIEVE IN YOU

Finally, dear reader, there is no such thing as the perfect ethical consumer, and that shouldn't ever be what we strive for. Frankly, it doesn't exist, and I'm certainly not it (and neither is that person who's constantly trying to sell you ethical clothing because it's sustainable when you probably don't need that top either). But being the perfect ethical consumer isn't the point.

Thinking about your consumption is.

Not all fast fashion is created equal, but all of it is aiding and abetting the global crisis. But with all the information I've presented in this book, you can probably understand why I'm not exactly rushing out to buy more. I can tell you I feel 150 percent better since I stepped off the fast fashion treadmill, because the conveyor belt of constant consumption didn't actually spark joy but it did spark low esteem, discontent, insecurity, and a general unfulfilled feeling. It gave me an adrenaline rush at the cash register, but usually when that rush was over I was left feeling empty inside (and so was my wallet). And I knew deep down that it was wreaking havoc somewhere else in the world, too. And my cognitive dissonance needed to stop. It was splitting me in two.

The ways in which our society places value on objects, while simultaneously devaluing the labor of others—based upon class, race, and station in life—has got us spinning around in fifty different directions, buying constantly to achieve an unobtainable goal that has been perpetuated by the same people you give your hard-earned cash to in exchange for their manufactured empty-promise goods.

THE INDIVIDUAL VERSUS THE COLLECTIVE

Few people change their habits overnight. And we, as individuals, can only do so much work in silo. The constant debate of individual over collective action rages on in various spaces. But I'm of two mindsets regarding how change will come about.

I realize that I don't change anything about the system when I alone say, "I'm not buying fast fashion anymore." I'm not superior to the next person because I have a bit more money in my pocket to pay toward my clothes (though I will argue that if you're a constant fast fashion consumer, you too could have a bit more money in your pocket if you quit). But when a bunch of us start to realize that we don't need to buy into these systems that harm us (and others, and the planet) or constantly buy even when we don't need to, that's when we get a movement toward collective change, through our buying power or lack of. I don't see any corporation responding to Aja Barber standing on her soapbox saying, "Hey, you suck." Instead, I see them responding to a bunch of us, roughly hundreds and thousands of us going: "Nah."

Or:

"Hang on, if I buy less stuff, then I could spend more on the things that really matter" (the kind of common sense you just don't see on billboards). Cycles change when many of us stop shopping like it's a competitive sport to vie with one another over who is dressed in the latest, latest, latest fad and then solely evaluate that person on whether they have succeeded. Rather than, say, what they actually talk about or whether they are a good person.

No one's going to make thousands of styles of dresses and operate on a fifty-one-season-a-year fashion calendar if the rest of us generally just slow our roll and lean into who we really are. That calendar has been sold to us, and we may have bought into it to fill our sense of inadequacy, but we can break this cycle. And I'd be willing to bet that, if you're reading this book, your privileges might be similar to my own. Maybe it's not doable to buy all sustainable designers all the time, but perhaps you're on your way to realizing that buying the way we used to buy isn't actually doable or desirable either. Those dresses you bought last year were only more affordable at the time because you knew you would have to buy five, ten, or twenty more. But you didn't have to: you could have bought one. Those items were more budget-friendly for you, but someone elsewhere in a less-Westernized country ultimately paid a steeper price.

Collectively, as we start to step out of and away from our habits in order to investigate our levels of consumption and to share our findings with one another, we will begin to heal ourselves from the inside, too. Your worth isn't the value of fashionable garments you wear or own, but the care with which you treat yourself (and others, and the planet) and the things you already have. Stop wanting more when you have enough. Because, let me say it so that the world can hear: you are enough. What you wear doesn't define you. What you do does.

> "Stop wanting more when you have enough. Because, let me say it so that the world can hear: you are enough. What you wear doesn't define you. What you do does."

Collectively, when we raise our voices, we can create change for ourselves, and we can demand change for our planet and the other humans who inhabit it. The problem is too many of us aren't really pausing before we hit "purchase" to ask ourselves if the item we're about to buy truly brings joy, or if the feeling of buying products is the actual joy we're seeking. Is the purchasing joyous or the purchase joyful?

LIVING IN INTEGRITY

Most things on this planet have a cost, even things that shouldn't (we should do something about that...clean air, drinking water, food, healthcare, shelter are all human rights in my book, and this is my book). I get pretty sick of people saying off the cuff that integrity costs nothing. That's patently untrue. Integrity actually costs everything if you stick to your guns on the things you care about (and make it very public that these are the things you do *indeed* care about).

This year I decided to keep a spreadsheet of the things I've said no to and list why. The two underwear brands that were in no way sustainable but had money to splash out on marketing? *Would have been a down payment on a house for me.* The brand that talked a good game but balked when I mentioned that they needed more marginalized people on the board in order for it to be a conversation with equity? *That's redoing a bathroom and kitchen in that house.* I quantify things in this way so that people can fully understand what the cost is of sticking to my guns in order to "change the game." And I also do it because others are getting those things while pretending we all play for the same team, while they give up absolutely nothing.

Everyone praises integrity, but they don't realize that no one can live off integrity. I'm in a fortunate position where the only real responsibilities I have at the moment are caring about myself. But I do notice others in similar positions to myself who don't pass the mic enough and sit things out enough, when perhaps they have more power and financial privilege to do exactly that.

In June of 2020 we saw tons of Black Lives Matter pledges (especially in online spaces) from those who claimed to have their eyes suddenly opened to the oppressions that still permeate so many of the systems we all frequent. There were a lot of pledges to do better. We see the same thing every time a new documentary comes out that reveals how damaging our consumer industries are on the world (particularly the Global South). Similarly, there is no greater co-opt of feminism than brands celebrating International Women's Day while those same brands straight up *refuse* to pay the majority of their garment workers living wages. But people overlook this simple fact. Every single year. People claim to have their eyes opened to something new, and then continue to buy and to participate in their old habits.

I've got news for people with power and privilege. Integrity often requires missing out on paychecks, and sometimes doing that publicly, because that's how you use your power—by refusing to be bought. It's not "call-out culture" to say, "Sorry, ____, I can't work with you anymore because you were involved in a recent disaster that harmed humans." It's not "calling out" to question some of the companies who you have previously worked with. But if no one's giving up anything (especially those with power), then **nothing changes**. Marginalized people cannot change these systems alone. But that's what accountability looks like, and that's how you use your privilege. Yes, it takes bravery, but if you're already the person who gets all the pie in some spaces, you're exactly the person who has the power to change the system by speaking up.

> "Yes, it takes bravery, but if you're already the person who gets all the pie in some spaces, you're exactly the person who has the power to change the system by speaking up."

I'm just going to say it: If all the able-bodied, cisgender, white women of the world joined the conversation in a legitimate way, while passing the mic and giving up power (meaning sitting out campaigns and asking companies both privately and *publicly* to do better), I truly believe we'd start to shift systems overnight. The truth is, I get tired of people complimenting my integrity while never asking the same of their peers.

If you're admiring my integrity but you're not asking the same of others who have more privilege and power than me, then you are just waiting for a marginalized person to change the world, while not asking those with more privilege to join the fight. And it's tiresome. Black women are not your mules.

People ask me how I got to this place where I am often saying no to thousands of pounds of work. It's certainly not that I can't use the money. But I've always believed that once your basic needs are covered, then you're fortunate. If you can buy a house where you want to live, then you're privileged. If you have food in your fridge, then you're privileged. If you have healthcare, you're very privileged (though healthcare should, frankly, be a human right).

After you make a certain amount of money and your basic needs are covered, plus you have a few fun extras (vacations, treating yourself to good things and enriching experiences, and the ability to care for loved ones), your levels of happiness are no different than the person with a billion dollars. That's part of why I've never gotten the billionaire thing. You can't take it with you, so while you're on this planet you may as well use it if you have it to improve the lives of others. Keeping it all for yourself feels frankly inhumane and also has a lot to do with how we have gotten ourselves into this whole mess. Having all *the things* doesn't actually bring joy.

I frankly didn't want *all* the money in the world. I began to think that once I reached a point where I felt comfortable and secure, that would be the moment where I started to say no and left the money on the table more and more. Sometimes it leaves me wondering why others refuse to do the same thing. I can't make their decisions for them, but I can call bullshit when others with more privilege than myself claim to care about the things that are harming *all of us*, all while leaving *nothing* on the table and never using their privilege to take a public stand.

Why is it important to talk about these things in public? Well, truth be told, a lot of shady business happens behind closed doors. People say one thing and do another. If everyone cares so much about these issues every time a building catches on fire and innocent lives are lost, then there's no harm in publicly having the conversation where you ask for more. Especially when you have leverage with corporations to force hands when it comes to demanding necessary change. The time for change was in the nineties when many of us became familiar with the term "sweatshop labor" for the first time. No more secrets and no more private chats about not harming innocent people and the Earth with your business practices.

It's one thing to tell that PR person in an email "no, thanks" and then pat yourself on the back for doing a "good" thing. It's another thing to say it publicly on social media. "I've worked with this brand in the past and I'm declining from this point on for these reasons, and I ask upon this brand to do better in the future and hopefully we can restore our relationship because I do like their products…but I don't like these sorts of actions that do harm for X, Y, Z reason."

One of these actions feels very safe and is the casual privileged-person way of maintaining the relationship while putting *absolutely nothing* on the line and ultimately maintaining the systems of power that harm others. The other is using power and leverage to force hands. I prefer people who participate in the latter. It's putting your money where your mouth is and demonstrating accountability to those watching who may not know how to do the same.

Asking for accountability is *not* the same as canceling a brand (even though I've heard this wimpy excuse every time). Canceling is basically going: "No one should ever buy from this brand again, they should not exist, I don't want them to survive." Accountability is simply asking that those with power do better. Please do not confuse the two. Asking hard questions from brands isn't canceling brands. It's accountability. Let's not get this confused. If it's time for all these conversations to be had, then why on Earth are we not having them in the open, in front of the general public? I think many still turf-guard and want to hold on to power, while aligning themselves publicly with the right message at the right time.

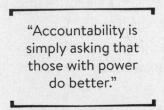

"Accountability is simply asking that those with power do better."

Earlier in 2020 a nameworthy brand got in touch with me about working together. I really weighed the pros and the cons.

The pros:

- Good money.
- An opportunity to have conversations with people in power and create actual change.
- An opportunity to carve out actual seats at the table for people more marginalized than myself. This one's the kicker. If you're walking into rooms and accepting seats at the table, but you know that people more marginalized than you are being left out of the conversation, you have an opportunity to hold the door open and let others come in with you.

Especially when we're talking about corporations worth billions of dollars.

The cons:

- This brand has taken a lot of heat for missteps with marginalized groups, so I would spend a lot of time explaining my decision.
- I'm at the point when occasionally I feel like people aren't asking me to work with them from a genuine place of improvement but more from a place of "pay her to shut the fuck up." And I can't put a dollar amount on me shutting up any time soon (smiles).

Weighing all of this, I decided to take the call and find out more information. During that call I came in with a list of "must haves" for myself in order to move forward with what was being proposed to me. We both went away. About a month later I received a letter of offer extending to me an opportunity to work with them. My "must haves" were mentioned at the very bottom and quietly declined after the money was waved in my face. So, I declined. If a person or company isn't listening to you this early into a potential partnership on the things that you want in order for it to be a fair working relationship, they have no plans of actually listening to you once you've signed a contract.

Do I want to punch myself in the vagina every time I pass on that amount of money? (Stares at small but cozy London flat.) *Of course I fucking do.* Is it important? *Yes, it fucking is.* But if I'm the person who can do that, why can't more able-bodied, cisgender, affluent, and privileged white people do the same thing?

(Because many people are still holding on to power, while continuing to align themselves with marginalized people publicly and yet still participating in systems that harm marginalized people.) It's a confusing headache, some of y'all.

The burden of integrity shouldn't be on the Black person. Or the working-class person. Or the plus-size person. Or the transgender person. Or the person with a disability. Someone who supports my work summarized a lot of my feelings about this. They said, "I think it was on [an Instagram] live that someone said integrity is a 'cost-benefit analysis.' Integrity costs more with each intersection of identity it crosses down the hierarchies of privilege/oppression, because reality is we can't opt out of capitalism all that easily but a cis het white influencer is losing out on less by turning down something influential on the grounds of integrity. Chances are they'll be offered something else sooner because of privilege. I know you hold yourself to very high standards and accounts and it's something we all should strive for but we (me, white people) have got to recognize the nuance of how much it costs different people to do that. It's so great you're having this conversation and totally sucks that you lose out on things that would help make life easier because companies are just paying lip service and not actually willing to change."

With that, I have a challenge for my fellow influencers, content creators, writers, activists, and anyone reading this book. How many things are we actually going to say no to this year, and why? Next time we read about some epic disaster where human life is lost, how many of us will take a stand and say, "Wow, I can't do this anymore, and here's why"?

I think it's time to realize that we're playing a part, too, and that there's power and privilege there. "Fast fashion" became a part of the everyday citizen's lexicon right about the same time "social media" did. The two are inherently connected, no matter which way you slice or dice it. That's why I don't sell clothing on my platform with the swipe-up mechanism. It aids and abets instant gratification without cross-examination.

I could sell a lot of stuff...if I wanted to. I don't. But let's break down the numbers here. If I sell something every day of the week in my stories and 1 percent of my readership swipes up to buy that item, that is 2,290 sold daily. Weekly, that's 11,450 items. Monthly, that's 45,800 individual pieces. And yearly...that's 549,600. And if I made a commission on all those products...frankly, I'd be rich. Now this clearly isn't the tale of every person with a platform, so take it with a grain of salt...but I'm sure some are pulling in these numbers easily.

Half a million pieces sold by one Instagram account, if only 1 percent choose to buy that product every weekday.

Now most brands govern influencers, so is anyone surprised that fast fashion sells so well?

So, let's put the cork in the champagne on the International Women's Day post if we're just going to go back to selling more stuff and exploiting...more women.

Maybe it's just time for more of us to say "no, thank you" and really mean it.

SUSTAINABILITY IN ACTION

It's important to realize where the roots of integrity and sustainability have actually come from. A community that relies on "just enough" as a collective can live in harmony with the resources around them. The people hovering around the poverty line and Indigenous people who use what they have and make do with less are the model. The cult of the individual is not: this cult constantly seeks to take too much, not out of need but out of want. No one who is really poor is going to run out or click through to PayPal and buy those bamboo storage containers because they saw them on Instagram. But they sure will if they are thinking how they appear, rather than what they can't live without. Other people are reusing a container that you might just throw into recycling. By necessity, they see worth in what we have been told to see as disposable (so that we keep consuming). Look for worth in the objects around you and in yourself. It's important to realize that sustainability isn't rushing out to buy "sustainable products." Sustainability in its purest form is being sustainable with that which you already own. And who you already are.

- It's making your stuff last by taking care of it and using it properly.
- It's questioning whether you actually *need* a new dress or if you *want* a new dress.
- It's thinking about whether you're "poor" or whether society's subliminal messages have made you feel lesser in order to lure you into the spend cycle because it has invalidated you and told you that your worth is only to be found externally through consumption, and not that you are valid and valuable in the first place.

So much of my past identity was wrapped up in consumption that I honestly couldn't visualize a world where I wasn't buying things to soothe my feelings or to help me feel less alone in my marginalized body that existed in a lot of white spaces. I had to unpack a lot of feelings before I truly stepped out of the cycle, and now I consider it one of the best things I've ever done for myself. Using my privilege for other things.

> "Sustainability in its purest form is being sustainable with that which you already own. And who you already are."

Because, truthfully, you have to have a certain amount of privilege to buy into these bad systems in such a repetitive way that you sustain them, especially in a world where most garment workers can't afford to buy the clothing they themselves produce. When almost half of humanity lives on $5.50 a day, it's very clear that not all of us are responsible for this mess. A lot of us are (but the billionaires are mostly), and yet we carry on playing a game we can't win.

The best solution is to recognize the cycles that you participate in and slowly remove yourself from them. And the next best thing we can currently do for this planet is to...wear our clothes. And chances are, if you're reading this, that's something you can participate in, and are probably (and hopefully) doing right this moment. After a year or two away from the cycle of buying weekly or monthly or every season, you will be surprised to find the ethical option wasn't that far out of your price range. Many of you have taken a breather because the global pandemic has caused us to shift our focus to other things. Good on you, keep that energy up. You can also champion a more diverse fashion landscape that caters to all bodies. It's not a movement if we continue to allow all the same barriers to limit who can participate.

And one last thing you can do—as you have almost finished this book and I am going to wrap things up fifteen minutes early so you have extra time on your hands—is to please write to or address lawmakers and brands to give us clothing and a fashion industry that we can all believe isn't completely extractive from start to finish. This is the *most* important bit. You can and should ask *more* of governments and corporations.

But in the meantime, what I do know and what I want you to believe in is that when a lot of us shift our mindset and decide to put our money in as many different directions as possible and wise up to the systems we feel compelled to participate in, even though we *don't even like them*...we become an unstoppable tidal wave. A force made strong by the sum of its parts.

Should this be on the customer?

Most likely not, but when the corporations start to feel more powerful than governments, we might be the only ones who can stop this system.

A while back, I was talking in my sleep, and according to my husband I shouted, "Remember my name, you rich bastard!" One day I hope they remember who we are and why we stopped buying their goods and their bullshit. And I hope they wish they had heeded our cry.

I hope this helps you to see and believe in your power.

Because I am ultimately rooting for you.

Rooting for all of us.

And I know you're going to feel better for it.

The global climate certainly will.

Go ahead and put that back on the rack. Remove it from your shopper basket.

You don't need it, because you're good as you are.

ACKNOWLEDGMENTS

For all the marginalized people doing the hardest work in the fashion industry. To the garment workers marching in the streets for fair payment and treatment. I see you. I fight with you.

To my wonderful husband, Stephen, thanks for riding out this with me, being supportive, and losing your dining room table to a book while taking some of my favorite photos. To my family, Mum, Dad, Ayana, and Aisha (Avery and Liam), I love you all so very much. I've missed you all this pandemic year. To the Cunningsworths (Isla and Bryn), my UK family, thank you for being so utterly welcoming. To Sofia, thank you for believing in me when I sometimes didn't believe in myself.

To all the women of color who contributed to this book or gave me your thoughts: Cleopatra Tatabele, Kalkidan Legesse (so glad I wandered into Sancho's that rainy day), Swatee Deepak, Anyango Mpinga, Dominique Drakeford, Samata Pattinson, Kimberly Jenkins.

To Rupert and Abi, thank you for being wonderful friends and taking a chance on a random kid from the States. My experiences with you changed the trajectory of my life. To Sue B, thank you for giving me a place to live those many years ago.

To Jon, Safae, and Zainab...you're a fantastic team, couldn't ask for better. To Romilly, I couldn't do it without you, thank you for seeing the value in this book. To Nana, I'm so glad you asked, thank you for your hard work.

To my friends Rabya, Rida, Kit, Lucy, Joemy, Lena, and Bo, I thank you for bravely stepping up on Instagram. Nothing about the fashion landscape there would ever change without you all. To Lora Nikolaeva for being an excellent designer and a wonderful friend. You make my fashion dreams come true. To Hanne K for making me take my own work and value seriously. To Katie Rispin for always being such a supportive friend.

To Gina Martin, thank you for being a consistent champion of others, including me. To Munroe Bergdorf...you continue to be a light to us all. Thank you to Dr. Ayana Elizabeth Johnson, who simultaneously makes me laugh and inspires me. To Audre Lorde and Dr. Kimberlé Crenshaw, who wrote the framework to which I examine the world today. To Ijeoma Oluo and Sam Irby, who have been consistently setting the path for many of us. To Quinta B for making me laugh. To Blair Imani for being a good friend. To Layla Saad for amplifying my work and believing in me, and Leesa Renée Hall for being a friend in the space.

To Slow Factory and Céline Semaan, thank you for believing in my work very early in and giving me a main stage to present it on. There is so much good that comes from the work you do. To the team at the OR Foundation for all the research and leading a foundation the right way, constantly striving to give back. To Nkemi, thank you for taking such good care of my house while

ACKNOWLEDGMENTS

I was writing this. To Judye Heitfield for the therapy that helped me get over my fears. And to Heather Redding for being so brave and inspiring constantly!

To my fashion industry peers who fight for a better and more fair industry always: Elizabeth Cline, Venetia LeManna, Orsola de Castro, Sophie Benson, Sophie Slater, Lauren Bravo, Kellie Dalton, Janelle Hanna, Livia Firth.

To Piper, I miss you so much. To my cats, Olive and Juno, get off the table.

HOW I HAVE EDUCATED MYSELF

BOOKS

All We Can Save: Truth, Courage and Solutions for the Climate Crisis, eds. Ayana Elizabeth Johnson and Katharine K. Wilkinson (One World, 2020).

The Body Is Not an Apology: The Power of Radical Self-Love, Sonya Renee Taylor (Berrett-Koehler Publishers, 2021).

Deluxe: How Luxury Lost Its Luster, Dana Thomas (Penguin, 2007).

Fashionopolis: The Price of Fast Fashion and the Future of Clothes, Dana Thomas (Penguin, 2020).

Fattily Ever After: A Black Fat Girl's Guide to Living Life Unapologetically, Stephanie Yeboah (Hardie Grant Books, 2020).

Fearing the Black Body: The Racial Origins of Fatphobia, Sabrina Strings (NYU Press, 2019).

How to Break Up with Fast Fashion, Lauren Bravo (Headline Home, 2020).

Overdressed: The Shockingly High Cost of Cheap Fashion, Elizabeth L. Cline (Portfolio, 2012).

Stitched Up: The Anti-Capitalist Book of Fashion, Tansy E. Hoskins (Pluto Press, 2014).

To Die For: Is Fashion Wearing Out the World?, Lucy Siegle (Fourth Estate, 2011).

USEFUL WEBSITES

allwecansave.earth

asia.floorwage.org

blackcotton.us

cleanclothes.org

concernedresearchers.org

eco-age.com

fashionandrace.org/database/vision-statement/

fashionrevolution.com

garmentworkercenter.org

theor.org

oxfam.org

payyourworkers.org

politicallyinfashion.com

remake.world

resourcegeneration.org

slowfactory.foundation

threadingchange.org

ONLINE CONTENT

"A New Textiles Economy: Redesigning Fashion's Future, 2017," Ellen MacArthur Foundation, http://www.ellenmacarthurfoundation.org/publications (Accessed May 6, 2020).

"Fixing Fashion: Clothing Consumption and Sustainability," Environmental Audit Committee, UK Parliament, https://publications.parliament.uk/pa/cm201719/cmselect/cmenvaud/1952/full-report.html#heading-11 (Accessed May 6, 2021).

Alexa Ream, Draven Peña, and Elie Fermann, "The Dream Will Never Pay Off: How Unpaid Internships Uphold Exploitation and Hinder Financial Sustainability within the Fashion Industry," Sustainable Fashion Initiative, Cincinnati, May–September 2020,

https://7312a40b-9e53-410d-a454-710337141387.filesusr.com
/ugd/70e175_4078c6302e1c4841a46417ecd0b2ba1d.pdf (Accessed
May 10, 2020).

PODCASTS

"Actions Make Movements: Labour Organising (Part 1)," *Remember Who Made Them.*

"Screaming into a Jar (aka Student Loans)," *Bad with Money with Gaby Dunn.*

SOCIAL MEDIA

"The Myth of Ethical Consumerism with Elizabeth Cline," The Sustainable Fashion Forum, https://www.youtube.com/watch?v=iZa9Utu8wnA&t=932s (Accessed May 6, 2020).

The Story of Stuff, The Story of Stuff Project, https://www.youtube.com/watch?v=9GorqroigqM (Accessed May 12, 2021).

The World's Most Polluted River, DW documentary, https://www.youtube.com/watch?v=GEHOlmcJAEk (Accessed May 10, 2020).

HOW YOU CAN EDUCATE YOURSELF

The list below are some of the most inspiring people and organizations who have educated me, and who I recommend you look up if you're interested in learning more about the issues raised in this book:

Anannya Bhattacharjee, Twitter: @AnannyaBhattach
    Union and social justice activist, International Coordinator
    for the Asia Floor Wage Alliance and President of the
    Garment and Allied Workers Union in North India.
Elizabeth Cline, Twitter: @Elizabethlcline
    New York–based journalist and author of *Overdressed: The Shockingly High Cost of Cheap Fashion* (Portfolio,

2012) and *The Conscious Closet: The Revolutionary Guide to Looking Good While Doing Good* (Plume, 2019).

Swatee Deepak, Twitter: @Swatee
Feminist activist, philanthropy advisor and co-founder of the *Remember Who Made Them* podcast.

Dominique Drakeford, Twitter @DomDrakeford
Sustainability and social justice impact influencer.

Roxane Gay, Twitter: @rgay
Writer, https://roxanegay.com/.

Kalkidan Legesse
Founder of Shwap.co.uk and Managing Director at Sancho's ethical clothing store, sanchosshop.com.

Anyango Mpinga
CEO and Creative Director of Anyango Mpinga womenswear brand, anyangompinga.com.
Also Founder of Free As A Human Foundation advocating the end of modern slavery and supporting survivors of human trafficking.

Ijeoma Oluo, Twitter: @IjeomaOluo
Writer and speaker, author of *So You Want to Talk About Race* (Seal Press, 2018), https://www.ijeomaoluo.com.

Céline Semaan, Twitter: @celinecelines
Executive Director and Co-Founder of Slow Factory Foundation, working at the intersection of climate and social justice, and fashion developments with adjacent industries such as waste, agriculture, education, and design.

Liz Ricketts, Twitter: @theORispresent
Co-founder and Director of the OR Foundation, theor.org.

INDEX

INDEX

INDEX